WINNING BY RESTING

SET YOUR PRAYER LIFE ABLAZE
SOAR IN VICTORY
SEIZE YOUR DESTINY

PAUL MOSES C. RATNAM

WESTBOW
P R E S S®
A DIVISION OF THOMAS NELSON
& ZONDERVAN

WestBow Press books may be ordered through booksellers or by contacting:

WestBow Press
A Division of Thomas Nelson & Zondervan
1663 Liberty Drive
Bloomington, IN 47403
www.westbowpress.com
1 (866) 928-1240

Because of the dynamic nature of the Internet, any web addresses or links contained in this book may have changed since publication and may no longer be valid. The views expressed in this work are solely those of the author and do not necessarily reflect the views of the publisher, and the publisher hereby disclaims any responsibility for them.

Any people depicted in stock imagery provided by Getty Images are models, and such images are being used for illustrative purposes only. Certain stock imagery © Getty Images.

All Scripture quotations, unless otherwise indicated, taken from the New King James Version®. Copyright © 1982 by Thomas Nelson. Used by permission. All rights reserved.

Scripture marked (KJV) taken from the King James Version of the Bible.

Scripture quotations marked MSG are taken from THE MESSAGE, copyright © 1993, 1994, 1995, 1996, 2000, 2001, 2002 by Eugene H. Peterson. Used by permission of NavPress. All rights reserved. Represented by Tyndale House Publishers, Inc.

ISBN: 978-1-9736-6202-0 (sc)
ISBN: 978-1-9736-6201-3 (hc)
ISBN: 978-1-9736-6203-7 (e)

Library of Congress Control Number: 2019906879

Print information available on the last page.

WestBow Press rev. date: 09/19/2019

Lovingly dedicated to my two great grandparents
who lived in the 1900s and have inspired me in my service—
Late Mrs. Anammamal, my paternal great
grandmother, who walked around
the villages in South India as a missionary
serving tirelessly against all odds, and
Late Rev. Daniel Perumal my maternal great
grandfather who is fondly remembered
as a man of faith, love and prayer.

Foreword

It is indeed an honor to write a foreword for Rev. Paul Moses C. Ratnam's book 'Winning by Resting'.

I know Rev. Paul as an anointed preacher, worshiper and great encourager of the body of Christ. Truly, God has called him to be a General for His Kingdom in this present time, and in the days to come. While his life clearly reflects the manifest power and glory of God, he still remains humble and compassionate. In reading this book, I could fathom the heart of the author, and perceive his close walk with our Lord.

The primary object of a person's prayer is not only to ask God for his needs, but also to grow closer in his relationship with the Almighty God. As I went through this book, it inspired me to draw closer to God in prayer, and thus find rest in God in the midst of all my problems.

As a reader, you will discover the depth and the importance of prayer as you read this book. The outcome will impact every area of your life. By the time you finish reading this book, I am certain your prayer life will be dramatically changed and you will be able to unlock God's fullest blessings for you.

May this book be a source of blessing to readers worldwide!

Samuel Mohanraj Ebenezer
Showers of Blessing Ministries,
USA

Acknowledgments

Dear Reader, I want to sincerely thank you for picking this book up amidst an ocean of writings and giving me an opportunity to serve you through what the Lord has bestowed in my hands to bless you.

I am so grateful to my darling wife Preetha—the kind of person you are—with your warmth, your love, and your support that you have shown thus far, and even in the many days of staying awake with me into the early hours of the day, as I wrote this book. Our children Joshua, Chris and Jeduthun—you never cease to touch Papa's heart for who you are. Love you "JCJ"!

Thank you Dad and Mom for your lives and commitment, and your faith in me to encourage me in my passion for kingdom responsibilities in my younger days. Thank you Matt and Moni for your support and prayers.

Thank you to the entire Team at the WestBow Press (a division of Thomas Nelson and Zondervan), each person whom I met along the way of getting this book out.

My sincere gratitude to beloved Bro. Samuel Mohanraj for your valuable guidance in many ways towards the completion of this book.

Thank you Jagan Prasanth and Vijay for your timely help. My appreciation to Latha Gideon and each one in the Fountain of Compassion ministry team for your sincere commitment to the ministry.

My heart goes out with special thanks to every intercessor who stood with me in this project and each faith partner of our ministry. I want to appreciate all the leaders and the congregation of the Fountain of Compassion church who stand together as we strive to carry the love of God to the hurting world around.

I want to thank You Lord with all my heart. I am eternally grateful to you, for drawing me to Yourself and teaching me Your word. Be glorified!

"Oh, how I love Your law! It is my meditation all the day" (Psalm 119:97).

Contents

Introduction

As we go through life, we all face times when our back is against the wall. Sincere efforts seem to fail and time ticks away. "Will I really make it?" Questions like this arise in the mind and life that once felt like "born to win" begins decelerating into survival mode–

A mother dealing with her difficult child, a young man fighting to see an open door in career, a family caught in the mire of misfortune, a business bearing the brunt of a collapsing economy, or a minister crying within saying, "Lord, when will that vision come true?" The list goes on and on. If your story is of someone like that, then *winning by resting* is for you.

As the children of Israel panicked before the Red Sea, Moses told them, "Stand *still*, and see the salvation of the LORD, which He will accomplish for you today. For the Egyptians whom you see today, you shall see again no more forever. The LORD will fight for you, and you shall hold your *peace*" (Exodus 14:13–14 emphasis added).

Though the armies of Pharaoh were behind them, Moses was reminding them that the outcome of the grim situation was not tied to their abilities or inabilities, but to the power of God. The Bible clearly states that these were not the words of God. These were the words of Moses, the servant of God. How could a mortal man be so full of confidence in a situation that could strike dead any man twice? Moses had discovered the power of *resting* in God. God was no more a distant spectator to him. He had reached a place in his *relationship* with God where God was active and would step into any crisis when there was the call of prayer. It is such relationship with God that produces rest.

Our victory is not the product of our credentials. It is the consequence of God's power present in our lives. But how did the Israelites tap into that power to win? How did they defeat the largest army of their time and go beyond the sea? Anything they would have tried to do at that moment on their own would have been in vain. They did not fight back. They did not take buckets full of sea water to try and make a way. They did not try building a bridge to the other side. Yet they won and the enemy plunged into the depths of the sea.

They saw the victory (salvation) of the Lord by standing still—by *resting* in God. Resting in God is not mere physical rest. It is not even trying to calm your mind, although that may be a consequence of resting in God. To rest in God is to trust in the nature of God and His promises with every fiber of your being. It is a state of such *abandonment* to God that heaven engages on your behalf. It is not a sensational trust. It is a trust that is built brick by brick on the altar of prayer. Such trust comes with a price of praying that engages the whole being of a person—spirit, soul, mind and body.

Right understanding of prayer is must if we should not despair in prayer. Prayer is not an *event* that happens at times of need. It needs to be an everyday action that is continuously practiced till a level of complete trust in God is reached. Usually, at a moment of such prayer, we get to hear the voice of God. It is that voice that opens our eyes to things that we have not seen thus far. It opens the invisible realm to us and gives us power over it. Our faith increases and a miracle is born!

We need to press through in prayer like Moses. He reached that place of unshakeable trust because of his communion with God through prayer, during the highs and lows of life. Even at the Red Sea, he *cried out* to God in prayer. He reached the place of rest in God. It was no more Moses' battle. It was God's battle. It was no more children of Israel versus the army of Egypt. It was the God of

Israel versus Pharaoh (Exodus 14:25). God instructed him to stop praying and lift up the rod to divide the Sea. When we reach that level of complete trust through prayer, God speaks. When Moses acted upon divine instruction, one of the most quoted wonders of the Old Testament was birthed: the Red Sea was divided (Exodus 14:15–16). This is: winning by resting.

The Bible is the book of supernatural and so is the Christian's life. God wants you to move into the realm of the impossibilities and explore the depths of His power and His glory. It happens by reaching the place of divine rest through prayer. In the pages of this book, I want to take you through a journey of dynamic truths on prayer and its power. It is my prayer that as we walk together across each chapter, you will be energized by the Spirit of prayer. You will be enabled by the truths to rise from the ashes and soar into the destiny that you were created for. That it shall be true of the words: where the man has failed, prayer *prevails*.

Chapter 1

THE REST CALLED "PRAYER"

It was an evening in September 2005. . . . Trichy, a city in South India . . . . An ambulance plying on the busy roads arrives at the hospital. . . The stretcher rolls out with an eighty-seven-year-old woman. She had suffered a massive stroke that had left her with paralysis in the left arm, left limb and a blinded left eye. Mrs. Elizabeth was my grandmother who had been a teacher during her younger days, and after her retirement, she had been serving the Lord in her own way as an intercessor and leading the women's ministry at Fountain of Compassion church. As they rolled the stretcher into the intensive care unit (I.C.U), I was walking alongside. Knowing her end was not far, she said to me in a frail voice, "Can you please fulfill my commitment towards the building project of the new worship sanctuary?" I assured her, "Yes Achi (that's how we called her at home), don't worry." I encouraged her that everything would be alright. But I knew that things were bad in shape.

The doctor examined her and shook his head in dismay. Her blood pressure was very high—270/180 mmHg. His words were: her situation is like a cat on the wall. She can collapse anytime or come back with her present state of paralysis. He said, "This is the beginning of the end". The treatment began. The next 24 hours were crucial. Too many things were running through my mind.

Will she make it? She was instrumental in helping me learning a lot of scriptures and songs during my childhood days. She had always dreamed of the day she would worship the Lord in the new sanctuary. But now, it was a humanly impossible situation. "She cannot die", I started telling myself. When everyone who came to see her had left after praying together that evening, I volunteered to stay in the hospital. I could not sleep. I began praying. There was a lot of burden in my heart, out of my love for her. After a while, I realized, that I was praying in the Spirit. Hours ticked away. It was 10pm, . 11pm. . 12 midnight, . 1am, . . My eyes were very tired . . But I would not want to quit, . It was as if a battle had been raging for her life. . 2am. . 3am. . And then suddenly, something happened. The presence of God became so strong around me. As my eyes fell on the name board of the room "I.C.U", in the Spirit I saw something else written, . . I See You. The experience was so strong that it brought such freshness to my mind as if a golden streak of the morning sunlight fell on me. I was quickly reminded of how God had heard Hagar's cry at Beer-Lahai-Roi, and opened her eyes to see a spring and Ishmael the dying lad lived (Gen. 21.19). I knew for sure in my heart that the battle was over and the victory won. I began praising the Lord.

When the morning arrived, the doctor was surprised that her blood pressure had come back to normal, and her arm and limb had regained their function. She was able to walk, talk, and use her hands. It was a miracle that brought joy beyond words. On the third day, her blind eye could see again. The doctor who was an ardent Hindu testified: God whom you serve had given her the miraculous healing. On her return to home, she lived to see the dedication and got to worship in the new sanctuary. It was winning by resting through the power of prayer.

Your First Response

> Let us go speedily to pray before the LORD, and to
> seek the LORD of hosts:

> –Zechariah 8:21 KJV

Prayer is urgent. It is the first action for any moment and the first aid that you need in any emergency. We need to stir ourselves up for prayer. For without prayer, nothing is possible. Prayer moves God. Prayer puts God to work. Prayerlessness prevents God from action and deprives a man of all help from God. Just like a soldier in the warfront without communication with the general is lost and becomes easy prey for the enemy, so is the prayerless one before the devil.

The kings of the Bible who knew the power of prayer made no delay in approaching God for any situation. They took the problem as it is to God to invoke divine intervention. They knew that the quicker they approach God in prayer, they could engage Him, His angels and heaven's armies in their affairs without delay. King Hezekiah entreated God when threatened by the army of Assyria. He prayed a heartfelt prayer in that moment of emergency that moved heaven. And an angel defeated the enemy killing 185,000 of them overnight (Isa. 37:14–36). Think about that number of warriors slain by one angel. This is the expanse of prayer! Let prayer be your first response to every situation you face. It is good not to waste time and strength trying all other avenues for solution before coming to God. It is a matter pertaining to wisdom to go to God first. You will find the answer after you have stepped into God's presence.

Paul Moses C. Ratnam

Real Rest Is to Wait on God

> Rest in the LORD, and wait patiently for Him; do not fret.
>
> Because of the man who brings wicked schemes to pass.

> —Psalm 37:7

It is important to stop to "power up" your life. It is like stopping your car at the fuel station to fill gas. Waiting on the Lord is an act of faith. It is not enough to have faith. You should put it to action. Waiting on the Lord produces spiritual giants. Many times it requires some sacrifice, the laying down of something that seems to benefit you. It is important to understand that being with the Lord could do much greater and long-lasting things.

It might seem a little inconvenient to take a detour and stop when you see the Master standing and waving at you from a distance. You feel the pressure of others chasing at full speed. The devil tries to tell you that you will lose the race and tempts you to go past the Master. If you go past, you miss Him. And you miss the purpose of life.

He is waiting with a plan and direction. He is waiting to fill you with power for action. When a traveler misses the map, the direction to reach the destiny is lost. What is the point in going past the petrol station without filling the fuel? The power to reach the destination is lost, and so the race is lost too. It is wiser to stop and wait on the Master to receive purpose and power. Do not compare yourself with others. You are unique. You are fearfully and wonderfully made. God's roadmap for your life is unique. Wait on Him! You are called to rest in His presence. Rest in Him. You need not struggle all the way. When you listen to His call to wait, you do not have to regret later. Rest in the Lord till every inner turmoil fades away and quiet strength abides in your heart.

Chapter 2

THE ART OF WAITING
ON GOD

The Making of Spiritual Giants

> But those who wait on the LORD shall renew *their* strength; they shall mount up with wings like eagles, they shall run and not be weary, they shall walk and not faint.
>
> —Isaiah 40:31

When everything else you do depletes the inner energy, there is one way to build strength and renew it. It is by waiting on the Lord. Many people think that taking time for prayer is for those few who have the gift of prayer. But it all depends on what lifestyle you want to have: a tired, hopeless one or the one in which you keep going higher all the time. The eagle is one of the special creatures mentioned in the Bible. It is strong and majestic. It sees the prey from a great height and goes for it with accuracy. It waits for the air current and climbs higher with less effort. It flies above the storm. Most of all, it spends time alone and renews itself. It lives a life that is not accessible to the enemy.

God likens His children to the eagle. He wants to renew your strength everyday. The way to start renewing is by waiting on the Lord. When you are feeling tired inside, it is time to jam the brakes and set aside a time for waiting on the Lord. Such pause from the regular chores of life is not going to make you lose anything. It is the only way you let God come and reign in your life. At the same time, you are energized for greater efforts and heights. You are ready to fight the battle with new strength. It pushes back the devil till he loses confidence.

Look at Jesus as a thirty-year-old Son of Man ready to begin the assignment of His life. He humbled Himself in the waters of baptism although He was without sin. He was filled with the Holy Spirit in the Jordan although He was conceived by the Holy Spirit. Then He had to wait in the wilderness for forty days although He was God in flesh. He fasted and prayed in the midst of wild beasts. Nothing could distract Him. In the end came the spiritual battle with Satan himself. The outcome of the battle revealed His set priorities for the rest of His ministry—His love for sustaining Himself by feeding on the word of God, His heart to never tempt the Lord God by crossing the lines drawn by His Father, and His zeal to see God alone to be glorified and worshiped (Luke 4:1–14). When the battle was over, the devil left shamed and defeated. Angels came and ministered to Him. That day was the beginning of heavy angelic activity in His ministry. It never ceased throughout the next three-and-a-half years. Above all, He returned from the wilderness with power. He was not the "carpenter's son" anymore. He manifested Himself as the Son of God with power (Rom. 1:4). He was the great eagle soaring high. Miracles began to happen wherever He went. His fame spread through the entire region.

Staying in His presence makes you receive your strength. Then you go on from strength to strength endlessly. Wiser are those who know the secret of waiting, for they shall never become tired. After waiting comes mounting and flying. Nothing can stop them. They move in regions unknown to the human mind. They are hidden from the devil's eyes. They do not know exhaustion because they know when it is time to get back to waiting. They are strong always, for waiting is a regular part of their lives like that of Jesus.

Out of That Emergency Prayer

> Let not those who wait on You, O LORD God of hosts, be ashamed because of me;
>
> Let not those who seek You be confounded because of me, O God of Israel.

–Psalm 69:6

God longs for a relationship with man. That is the paramount reason that He created us. Any relationship needs to have a two-way communication to stay healthy and growing. The Bible on the whole talks much about prayer. Prayer is communicating with the Lord. And we hear from God by waiting on Him.

Waiting on the Lord is more than what many think as prayer. It is approaching God not just in a sense of emergency, but seeking Him unhurriedly and openheartedly. Waiting on the Lord is the time when we speak to God and God speaks to us. For God, it is the time when He finds a man to work *on* and work *with* to fulfill His purposes on earth. And for man, it is a time to *know* God's heart and His glory. There is no disappointment when you wait on the Lord because it is not a time to press in personal agenda but to be transformed. Your face is turned radiant as you wait on the Lord. There cannot be shame in your life. God has a great plan for your life. The right way of going high is to go high in prayer. Waiting does not mean wasting. Never! Failure comes when a saint confuses the priority of prayer with work.

Waiting demands time. There are other things that are waiting

7

to take your attention and pushing you to demand action. It requires a great boldness on your part to decide to take the time needed to wait on the Lord. It is a sacrifice that others may chide you for. You need the courage to wait on the Lord. It is a holy boldness that pays rich dividends later.

> Wait on the Lord; be of good courage,
>
> And He shall strengthen Your heart; Wait, I say, on the Lord!

> —Psalm 27:14

People who have not understood the power of prayer cannot pray. Those are the ones who decry prayer. The attitude to underestimate the power of prayer is the attitude of the flesh. The flesh wants to live independent of God by its own energy and strength. It is rebellious like an unbridled mule, not willing to wait on the Lord. We should not allow such thoughts to creep into us, for they make a person's life spiral down. Such a mind-set should be sent to the cross. It should be crucified until we find our complete abandonment to God. We should wait for heaven's limitless strength.

The sorrow of the disciples put them to sleep in Gethsemane. Their fleshly zeal to stand for Christ was too weak to stand in the face of trouble. It pushed them into cowardly denial of the Son of God. But Jesus had the boldness to wait on His Father. The whole of hell that fought against Him could not move Him. His heart was strong. He won Calvary's victory at Gethsemane. Truly Gethsemane was His *battlefield* and Golgotha His *victory podium*. Your prayer time is your battle time. The man who wrestles in prayer before God flies high in life's situations. Before the high priests, He spoke the truth that He indeed was the Messiah (Luke 22:69). There was no compromise in values. Herod's mockery could not move Him. He opened not His mouth (Luke 23:8–9). He was too strong. His strength humbled Pilate when He said that His Father was in control (John 19:11). Every effort to distract Him from the "mission to rescue mankind" failed miserably. All of these happened because He waited on His Father and was strengthened in Gethsemane. Do not fight for situations to change. Wait on the Lord and bring the change.

Closer to His Heart

> I waited patiently for the LORD; and He inclined to me, and heard my cry.
>
> —Psalm 40:1

Through prayer, God lifts us into a greater understanding of His nature. Sometimes the answers come immediately, but there are other times it takes longer. There is much supplication needed. You need to press through with your heart in such times of silence. It is like the horse that keeps its pace in the race even after it has lost its capacity to breathe. Be diehard! Much repetition and wrestling before Him must be done before the answer comes your way. Sometimes these questions might arise: Why can't God answer every prayer the same way? Is He not omnipotent?

The primary objective of prayer is to get us closer in our relationship to God. Everything else is secondary, although the Scripture does not underestimate the supplying of needs. We do not pray only to get things done. That might be a child's way of understanding prayer. We pray to see our heart beat with the rhythm of His heart. Get to the place where you *think* the thoughts of God. His thoughts are the very best. You can never improve on them.

Children can be asking daddy for things cheaper than what daddy wants to give them. When they wait, they mature to understand the heart of the Father who wants to give them good things. True prayer is to know God's will, desiring and asking for it, because of the conviction that there could be nothing better. When prayer is viewed as a relationship, the need to compel God for a selfish reason is lifted away and prayer becomes a quest to be satisfied by divine purpose. The psalmist learned that patient waiting in prayer causes God to incline. Should God incline for a mortal's cry? Yes, He does out of love. It is like a formidable heavyweight wrestler lovingly bending to embrace and kiss his son. It is power that is melting down by love.

With increased persistence in prayer, God's heart is brought to the closest reach. There comes the exchange of loving words, passionate gestures, and strong convictions between God and us. His ways and thoughts are as high as heavens. Such a lifetime of heavenly fulfillment begins when you are waiting before the Lord.

It Begins with a Choice

> But one thing is needful: and Mary has chosen that
> good part, which will not be taken away from her.
>
> –Luke 10:42

You always make the choice. There is no pressure. With choice comes responsibility. God takes responsibility when we choose what God wants us to. We become responsible for whatever we choose away from God. Martha and Mary were sisters who lived in the same house in Bethany. While Martha invited Jesus to her home, Mary sat at the feet of Jesus listening to His heart. While Martha focused in serving Jesus, Mary was giving her time to listen to Jesus. In a while, we see that the woman who invited Jesus into the house had lost her purpose. She began to get "distracted" in doing many things. She then complained to Jesus, the Guest. Martha tried to impose her frustration on Jesus. It is a sad thing to see the one who should have received the maximum joy is now reeling under the sting of self-pity. She did not understand the heart of the Master.

Jesus could have even had a late meal, for His bread was the will of the Father (John 4:34). When Mary sat at Jesus' feet opening her heart to receive what Jesus wanted to give, she was doing the "one needful thing". She was receiving an *impartation* of the heart of Jesus. She was receiving the good part. The good part is the fountain of blessing that will never run dry. It stays on. It will never be taken away. You pray and go. But the power of your prayer *lingers*. It goes beyond time to bless. After all, Jesus did not come all the way for a dinner. He came to impart life. Martha *invited*, but Mary *inherited*.

Later on, Lazarus the brother of Martha and Mary became sick and died. When Jesus came to Bethany after some days, we see Jesus going past Martha's lament. But Mary fell at the feet of Jesus. They were the same feet that she had waited upon. He was moved to tears when Mary wept. The Creator Himself wept at the tears of Mary (John 11:20–44). He raised Lazarus to life. It doesn't end there. It becomes sweeter later. The same Mary anointed His feet with the costly perfume honoring Him with her lifetime savings (John 12:3–7). Jesus assigned Mary's service as a prophetic confirmation of His death and accepted it as His burial honor. Unlike Martha, Mary gave Him more than a meal. She gave Him undiluted honor because she had a revelation of who Jesus really was. She made full use of the privilege of worshiping the Son of God as the "King" like the three wise men from the East. She gave something that would last forever. Real prayer lifts us from the realm of human opinions concerning God to see Him as He is—the One who reigns from the throne, Strong and Powerful!

Loving Him Deep Enough

> For since the beginning of the world men have not
> heard, . . nor has the eye seen any God, besides You,
> Who acts for the one who waits for Him.

> –Isaiah 64:4

Waiting is a great sign of love. You do not mind waiting for someone whom you love. In the Bible, the story of a crazy young man runs like this: Jacob was in love with the woman of his dream. But he was deceived by his uncle Laban and given in marriage to Leah. Did he give up? No. There was a new condition laid down by his father-in-law to serve seven more years for Rachel, his second daughter. Jacob chose to wait and work for Rachel. Those years seemed like days because of his love for her (Gen. 29:20). That is the 'waiting' power of love. Apostle Paul cites Isaiah 64:4 in his epistle to the believers in Corinth. He writes, "for them that love Him" (1 Cor. 2:9). Waiting is a powerful *evidence* of loving someone. God-waiters are God-lovers.

A man who prays loves God. Therefore he is willing to wait in prayer. It is strong, fiery love. It is love in action. A man who does not pray does not love God in reality. Let him not claim that he does, because he is not willing to prove his love by waiting. His love is like that of Peter who said that he loved his Master and would go with Him till death. But his action denied it. Prayerless love for God is far from love at all. It is shallow, emotional love. It is the kind of love that might say, "Lord, I am ready to go with You, both to prison and to death", but denies before a young maid's threat (read Luke 22:33). In Gethsemane, Peter did not pray in all the three times when Jesus exhorted Him. He denied Christ thrice before the rooster crew that morning. It is important we heed the voice of the Spirit who calls us to pray. No matter wherever you are, lift your heart and pray when He beckons you to pray.

Later on, we see Peter's love for waiting on God changed drastically. After the Pentecost, when there was a hassle in the church about stewardship, Peter the chief apostle made a strong exhortation that he along with the other apostles desired to wait on the Lord more than getting involved in things pertaining to service (read Acts chapter 6). There is another striking instance of Peter's change in his attitude in the book of Acts. He was staying in Joppa at the house of Simon the tanner. There was one afternoon when he was unusually hungry. But he preferred waiting on the Lord in prayer than going for lunch (read Acts chapter 10). Peter had reached the place where his hunger for prayer superseded his hunger for food. It was on that day that God opened Peter's eyes and showed him something awesome: he was to reach the gentiles with the gospel. Later when he obeyed the Spirit's bidding, he became the apostle to harvest the firstfruits of the gentiles at the house of the Roman centurion Cornelius. Another unusual thing followed that day. The Spirit of the Lord fell on the people who were listening to the preaching of Peter and they magnified God speaking in tongues. In those days, to receive the Holy Spirit while hearing a sermon was totally unheard of. Waiters on God are entitled to *first-of-its-kind* miracles.

Those who wait on the Lord with love are His chosen, special people. He prepares special blessings for them. They are allowed into His treasury to handle things that no one else could. God takes pleasure in giving them what He would never give to anyone else—all because they care enough to wait upon Him. Praying men and women are the only ones who value and respect the greatness of God.

> And therefore will the LORD wait, that He may be gracious unto you, . . . Blessed are all they that wait for Him.
>
> –Isaiah 30:18

We wait on the Lord who waits for us. As we go to pray, let us remember that God waits. It is a piece of truth we ought not overlook. Why should God wait? Many times the Bible connotes the waiting of God. He waits that all could be saved. He is long suffering. But here He does the waiting to show us that He cares. He knows all about us. He can do things instantly. Yet the Bible says, "That you check up on them every morning, looking in on them to see how they're doing?" (Job 7:18 MSG). God is visiting us everyday. He graciously enquires our wellbeing and listens to our cries not only to relieve our burdens, but to show us that He cares to understand. We find a true Friend in Him, if only we would speak to Him.

One of the moving scenes in the Scriptures, where we see the waiting of God is when Abraham was tested on mount Moriah. It is amazing to see how God waited and set everything up for that day to show that He longed to understand Abraham. It had been a long wait for God since He called Abraham when he was seventy-five years old. He had walked almost 4 decades with God with many ups and downs in his relationship. Though God knows us completely, He wants us to reveal our love for Him through the choices we make. Abraham had left His father's house. He had released his rights in the land to have peace with his brother Lot. He even released his past mistake and guilt by sending Hagar and Ishmael away in obedience to God. God saw Abraham through each of this *letting go* experience. It would have been hard for Abraham. But Abraham was a man who loved God from his heart in spite of his failings. Yet God was waiting for Abraham's greatest response, so that He could bless him forever. One day God called Abraham to sacrifice his beloved son Isaac. At that moment, Abraham displayed the same level of obedience that He had when he was called forty years ago. God's waiting came to an end. He said, ". . for now I know that you fear God, since you have not withheld your son, your only son, from Me" (Gen. 22:12). Heavens opened and blessings rolled over Abraham and his seed. God was so moved that day that it made God the Creator swear by Himself to a man (Heb. 6:13).

God was waiting for a day as such. When Abraham responded, God blessed him.

It touches our hearts to discover that God is waiting for us to receive our love. Much can happen when you wait for Him. He is moving you from one level of love to another like Abraham. When you reach each level of love for God, you are tested. Blessings flow because of your obedience. It is not how perfect we are, but how much love we can give Him.

On the other hand, He waits to perform to you what He has in store for you. It is much encouraging to know He is waiting for the right time to decorate your life. "He has made everything beautiful in its time" (Eccles. 3:11). We always think about our waiting and we become tired. We talk a lot about it. May we not ignore the waiting of God. God waits! It is for the manifestation of greater glory. When Jesus waited over the sickness of Lazarus, it was for a greater glory— raising of the dead man. God waited forty years in the desert for the Israelites to trust Him 100 percent. They misunderstood God's waiting while they hurried to escape from the desert. Let us not waste the waiting of God as many do. Know that He is merciful. As you grow in understanding His waiting, and respond to Him, you receive the reward. You shall be enlisted along the heroes of faith and be called "blessed" when you have fulfilled the purpose of His wait. You will be the fig tree that bore fruit for the Master and pleased Him for all the efforts He had poured into you.

Chapter 3

CULTIVATING THE PRACTICE OF PRAYER

During the early days of my ministry, on a fine morning, I was starting my day at the office. I had been writing articles for our ministry bulletin. We were supposed to send the church magazine for print. The messages I used to write brought in encouraging testimonies. To confess, I started allowing the busyness of ministry rob the place of prayer. During that time of the year, my prayer times had been inconsistent. It had dwindled gradually. Though I had a feeling that I had to set it right, the pressures of working *for* God was pushing me away from being *with* God. It was a week that my prayer time had almost hit the rock bottom. Ministry was going through lot of challenges. My health was frail. The need to keep up the pace in ministry was staring at me.

Being at the office early, I was alongside the staff for the printing of the final master page of the magazine. We were already beyond deadlines. We were late. I just wanted to see this last thing done and send it for printing. I wanted to finish things and go to pray. But it simply does not work that way always. The printer machine would not print. We tried. With a bit of my professional background in electronics, I did everything possible to sort it out. It started printing out junk. I was muttering but would not give up. We spent a couple of hours wasting time, paper and energy. It was of no avail. I was frustrated right in the middle of serving God. It was almost like the printer staring at me like Balaam's donkey and saying: you never waited on God. You can never do it on your own. I was convicted. I was broken in heart. Leaving the work as it is, I started to seek the Lord. It was the day I had learnt a life-lesson the hard way. Most importantly, that day I learnt that there is no *peace* in life without the *practice* of prayer. We might be missing out that peace at home, office, business or ministry. It might be health, finances or anything in life where we are struggling. Instances like this can happen to us frequently to remind us the importance of prayer. They are 'wakeup calls' from heaven.

Prayerlessness Is Absolute Helplessness

> My soul, wait silently for God alone; for my
> expectation is from Him.

> –Psalm 62:5

There is no other way things could happen for a child of God but through prayer. When you do not pray, life is lived at the mercy of blind fate. We need to be told this till we are convicted, thoroughly convinced, and controlled by prayer. We need to realize that there is no help available to us from God without prayer. The man who does not pray denies God's help. As rude as it may sound: he will not be helped. He cannot be helped.

Even in the innermost recesses of our hearts, let it be echoed to us that there is no answer that we may receive from God except through prayer. If answers come any other way, it is sure that they are short-lived. It is not going to keep us close to the heart of God and bless our lives continually. That would be a greater loss! We need to be thoroughly brainwashed on the subject of prayer that we dare not move on without it. Prayer keeps us at the place of safety because it keeps us dependent on God. Our life consciously begins to revolve around Him. We realize that it takes God to be what we are supposed to be and do what we are supposed to do. We shudder at the thought of venturing out on our own, no matter, how promising it may seem. Like the psalmist, we see God as our only hope. And He never fails. In battles, we look to Him for strength. In sorrow, we look to Him for peace. In pain, we look to Him for comfort. Everything that happens and that does not happen drives us to the one location—God. When you find Him, you find everything. When we become people who pray, we do not move without God. And we do not move to places where God does not move. Being God-carriers, we are hope-carriers to a brokenhearted world.

We need to ask God to birth in us a *reverence* about the importance of prayer. We need heaven's help to see prayer like the air and water for our physical bodies. We should have the boldness to even *ask* God to chasten and discipline us, if He would, till we have learnt to completely depend on God through prayer. Saints are made thus.

When a Helpless Man Denies Help

> Then He said to them, "My soul is exceedingly sorrowful, even to death. Stay here, and watch with Me."

> —Matthew 26:38

Sorrow is a neutral factor that can bring opposite consequences upon the choice you make. Jesus' soul was exceedingly sorrowful, even unto death. "And being in agony He prayed more earnestly" (Luke 22:44). When you have known that prayer is the way to escape and it is the only way, you don't do anything but pray. This is exactly what Jesus did. Look at the disciples, "He found them sleeping from sorrow" (Luke 22:45). What pain must have pierced through the heart of Jesus!

There is no excuse for not praying. Nothing can cover up for the lack or the absence of prayer. The man who does not pray bears the brunt of prayerlessness. He is wholly responsible for his prayerlessness. It is time to stop playing the *blame game* and get to pray. Prayer is the way out of any situation. It is available to anyone who would pray. Problem is not an excuse for not praying because not praying in the midst of trouble would be the biggest problem. It is willingly denying the choice to escape. No help could be rendered to the man who prays not. When a helpless man denies help, it is folly. No excuse can justify the cause for not praying.

It needs to be retold until it becomes a reality. Only God's arm can reach that unreachable answer, and prayer moves the arm of God. Real answers and lasting answers have to be answers to prayer. Prayerless work is the most dangerous risk. You can pray at the expense of work but not vice versa. Do not neglect prayer for anything. Let not your prayer life become an expense for anything. Ignoring prayer for work is an *expensive* mistake, for prayerlessness brings frustration and messes up our plans. When the devil sees a prayerless saint, he will finish him easily. A prayerless saint is a disarmed warrior. "Too busy to pray" is an invitation card delivered at the devil's doorstep to come and wreak havoc.

Prayer activates the realm of supernatural. Prayer takes you to the regions where the devil cannot touch you. You walk in the high realms of glory untouched by the forces of the world and the temptations of the archrival. You live before the throne of God in His power and wisdom. We need to realize that everything we do is in vain till we have prayed and engaged God into it. Nothing is done until we have prayed before doing it. We need to *conceive* plans in prayer, *nurture* them in prayer, *birth* them in prayer and *protect* them through prayer. The cause of all productivity and the source of all prosperity is God alone. Without inviting Him to be the Lord of what you do and asking Him to lead, whatever done is not done the way it ought to be. May we never take on the risk of prayerlessness. It might work one day but not always. If we passed a day peacefully without the hour of prayer, let it make us ashamed of our folly that we do not repeat such ignorance the next day. If our prayerlessness is convicted by the trouble of that day, may we humble without delay to get back to the place of prayer. Knowing this Jeremiah prays, "Are there any among the idols of the nations that can cause rain? . .Are You not He, O LORD our God? Therefore we will wait for You, since You have made all these" (Jer. 14:22).

First, Be with Him

> Then He appointed twelve, that they might be with Him, and that He might send them out to preach,

> –Mark 3:14

How many ever know that the number one qualification to be a disciple of Jesus? How many can say that they have it? Everyone who belongs to Him and who represents Him to the fallen world is expected to do this. When so many followed Christ everyday, why did He choose only twelve? He chose that they would be with Him, before the sunrise and after the sunset—to be with Him always How can He send those who have not been with Him? Those who are not with Him cannot represent Him for they have not known Him personally. Being with Jesus is ministering to Him and letting Him minister to us. We never learn ministering to Him until we have allowed Him to minister to us.

Those who had been *with* Him are the ones sent *by* Him. He does not send them empty handed with raw zeal. What can raw zeal do? Nothing. When He sends, He gives them power saying,

"Behold, I give you the authority" (Luke 10:19). Pitiable are those whom He does not send—who go out by themselves by their zeal. Prayerlessness makes for ignorant people. They expect the move of God but would destroy it when it arrives because they do not recognize it. God's movements begin *with* God and not *for* God. The prayer-less Peter sliced the soldier's ear for Jesus and grieved Him. He did not understand what His Master stood for. He misrepresented Jesus (John 18:11).

Spending time with the Lord everyday should be done in an attitude of openness. Open your mind and your spirit to what God wants to deposit in you. He does it through His word and the voice of His Spirit. When the disciples had tarried for ten days in the upper room, after the ascension of Jesus, the Spirit of God came upon them as cloven tongues of fire. He imparted the life and the power of Jesus into them. They were no longer the ignorant and weak fishermen. They became bold for God. Their boldness did not come with the sword or weapons. It came through the assurance of God's power in their lives. They did irrefutable signs and wonders that the society called them as people who "turned the world upside down". One thing became very clear to the world of their times—"they had been *with* Jesus" (Acts 4:13, emphasis added).

Even the Lesser-Sensed, They Pray

> The eyes of all look expectantly to You, and You give
> them their food in due season.
>
> —Psalm 145:15

Do you depend on God for your survival? Prayer is all about depending on God, being with Him, and working with Him. All fowls of the air, beasts of the land, and creatures in the sea wait upon the Lord every day for their survival. They know two things: God is their *only Provider*. Having known that, what they need cannot come by their own or by anyone else. They wait for Him. Second, they know that there is a *due season* for their answers. What revelation they have concerning God! They know in their innermost beings that there is no survival apart from God. Many times, man seems to be the only creature foolish enough not to realize his need for God.

The materialistic world has driven men and women away from God. People think that it is below their standard to utter 'God' in their conversation. By walking away with such independence, men have crushed themselves far below those lesser-sensed creatures. They deprive themselves of all the resources that come from God, who is the author of life. It cannot be so with the people who know God and are saved by Him. Let nothing in your life take your dependence away from God. Prayerlessness is the sign of independence. The young lions and whales pray. Lion is called the king of the jungle and whale is the massive creature in the sea. They pray in absolute need before God. How much should you and I pray? Happy are those lives where prayer *rules*, for they *never* run out of answers.

Chapter 4

PROMISES ON PRAYER

Being overwhelmed by the financial needs of an upcoming worship event that we were organizing, I was sitting in my room being pounded with anxious thoughts. God had put the desire in my heart to organize a mega worship event in our city. We had stepped out in faith. But going into details, I found things were getting complicated than how it looked from the surface, especially the finances. I did not want to retreat. God had given the vision. And it would surely bless the city. The question about money that is needed was the hard question on my mind that day.

Barely three weeks before the event, with just one-tenth of the total money in hand, the pressure was palpable. I decided not to approach anyone to lend. God had to do it. It was His ministry. It was His vision. I put aside the anxiety by *switching off* my mind and got to pray. God had taught me years before to switch off the mind when things got too difficult. *Prayer wins where reason has failed*. I was praying and praying. The reason of the prayer was desperation. If God would not do it, it could not be done otherwise. If the finances were not going to come, the event was not going to happen, and there is going to be shame. "O God, hear me!", I prayed. I prayed in the known tongue and I prayed in the unknown tongue moved by the Spirit of God. After a couple of hours, the sun had begun to set, and I heard something in my heart. It was so clear as if I heard someone sitting next to me saying, "All is done." It was an interesting phrase—all is done. I knew in my heart that the answer has arrived. Peace filled my heart. I was rejoicing and I spent a few minutes in giving thanks. Being moved by the Lord to give what I could, I decided to sell the wristwatch I used to cherish for the past nine years. That Sunday in a special auction held to raise money for the meeting, somebody came forward to buy that wrist watch for an unimaginable price—twenty times the actual cost of it. That was the power of God! To cut the story short, there was supernatural provision from every side, and that worship event became an unforgettable testimony to bless thousands of souls both in our city and beyond.

The Promise with Assurance

> Call upon Me in the day of trouble: I will deliver you, and you shall glorify Me.
>
> —Psalm 50:15

Premise: Premise is basis, ground and foundation. "Call upon Me in the day of trouble." When worldly help withdraws itself, the promise God makes is shaking. The ground is prayer. Prayer is the fuel that runs the vehicle of life, the signal that connects the warrior with the general. It is the vital sign that proves that the inner man is alive and well. Prayer is solid ground amidst a world of sinking sand. When you get to pray, heaven's attention is riveted to you, hell stop its advance, and time gives way to eternity, miraculous answers arrive, destruction is stopped by preservation, and a great door of opportunity presents itself right in the place of adversity.

Promise: "I will deliver thee." There is deliverance and answer. There is no doubt or confusion about it. The praying man is freed and there is no ambiguity. The praying man is facilitated, enabled and released. God comes down from heaven for the rescue. Be it the lion's den of Daniel, the fiery furnace of the 3 Jewish young men, the swallowing mire that Jeremiah was cast into or the prison where Peter was kept. He will send the angel to shut the lion's mouth, to douse the flame, lift you out and open the iron doors. It is done when prayer is in place. It cannot be done otherwise.

Praise: "You shall glorify Me." The promise comes with this assurance. What should be your response to the answer? The aftermath of a miracle is praise and worship. In fact it should start early like the praise of Paul and Silas because breakthrough is not denied for a man who prays. God has to be exalted high for who He is and what He does. The moment you begin praising God is the very moment you begin to receive the answer. If prayer is *asking*, praise is *receiving*. Praise unclogs the channel of blessing. With generous praise, answers rain down.

Escape Tribulations

> Watch therefore, and pray always that you may be
> counted worthy to escape all these things that will
> come to pass, and to stand before the Son of Man.

> –Luke 21:36

Here is a glorious promise that holds the key for all the protection you need for the rest of your life. God is getting ready to pull down the curtains on the stage of life. Sin, sickness and tribulation escalate; moral values are on the decline; uncertainty is the order of the day; disappointment rules in hearts everywhere. How are we going to face these dark days before the end? This is the question I too had when I first read the Book of Revelation. There is a way-out!

When Jesus was talking about the end time tribulation, He

said it would be such a difficult time since the world began. But still He was showing a way out for the faithful ones— watch and pray always that you may have the strength to escape tribulations and stand before the Son of Man. There is worthiness both to escape tribulation and partake in the "rapture". Watching and praying is the way of escape from temptations, trials and tribulations. To watch is to be alert. A watchman needs to be alert. Being alert is being sensitive to the Holy Spirit and picking His signals so that you engage in prayer. There are two ways of watching: one is when you see certain things happening around you and you feel the urge that you have to get to pray. It may be an attack in your family, on someone's spiritual life, health or finances. You don't just go past reasoning it away in the natural realm alone. You have to be alert spiritually and start seeking the Lord for the same. You need to *stand* in the gap and *close* the gap. You intercede and pray for cleansing and protection. You take it serious because it may be a symptom of something deeper that the Holy Spirit is showing you. Or it could be a signal of a major assault that the devil has planned. So it is important to watch and pray.

Secondly, when you sometimes feel disturbed or peaceless in the spirit, do not just take it light. Peace is the referee God has given us (Col. 3:15). When peace leaves us, it may well be the Holy Spirit setting off the alarm in you asking you to pray. Be quick to act. Begin praying right away wherever you are. Pray sprinkling the blood of Jesus. Pray in the name of Jesus demolishing every plan of the enemy against your life, family and those you are connected with. Pray in the Spirit till you feel the peace restored in your heart. God will release a word for you. You will soon hear the work of the Lord through a testimony. You may even see it with your own eyes.

It is not a surprise that God so highly values prayer. The reason is simple: Prayer gives us direct contact with God and it is the only strong proof of our dependence on Him. Prayer and sin cannot go together. Prayer and weakness cannot go together too. Prayer makes you spiritually alert and powerful.

It is time to bend your knees in prayer if you ever need *escape*. Get rid of false satisfaction, amusements and assuming false responsibilities. It is time to ask forgiveness for the sin of prayerlessness. Come on your knees before God in prayer. He shall keep you safe physically, spiritually and morally.

Turning Impossibilities Around

> Call unto Me, and I will answer you, and show you
> great and mighty things, which you do not know
>
> –Jeremiah 33:3

This is a verse when quoted without the context will make one feel that Jeremiah was part of an ongoing revival. No! He was imprisoned by king Zedekiah for prophesying Judah's doom because of its iniquity (Jer. 32:2). Jeremiah was given a piece of bread daily (Jer. 37:21). He became a political criminal hated by everyone. In such a place of obscurity was God meeting His man with this marvelous promise, "Call unto Me and I will answer you, and show you great and mighty things."

God saw that Jeremiah was in the prison cell. Though God knows everything, His promise might seem to be confusing at times. He speaks too great things when there is absolute impossibility. We need to understand that in divine dynamics, there is only one step between possibility and impossibility. It is the step of *faith-filled* prayer. It is the step of believing and acting in prayer. A little further beyond the thin veil of impossibility is God's avenue into the miraculous. When God removes the veil, impossibility turns into possibility. There is no impossibility associated with God. God is a Specialist who cancels out every human verdict of impossibility. So let it be also said that there is no impossibility for the praying man.

Prayer is *the* thing that God expects of a man who appears

to be cornered. God's action would be threefold for the praying man. There is an *answer*. Every mystery gets solved at the onset of wholehearted prayer. Prayer fuels your hope and gets you to the end of the tunnel. Adversity is transformed into opportunity. Great and mighty things happen as a result of prayer. Prayer is the doorway to the *miraculous*. Finally, prayer takes you beyond the realm of human *reason*. Jeremiah was delivered from the prison and set free because God made him find favor in the eyes of the enemy. No one can comprehend the beauty of an answer from God. He says: call unto Me!

He Shall Hear My Voice

> Evening, and morning, and at noon, I will pray, and
> cry aloud, and He shall hear my voice.

> —Psalm 55:17

The man who has learnt to cast every single concern that comes upon his heart to God has no problem praying three times a day or hours together (Ps. 55:22). He has found a friend in God that minutes give way to hours, and hours to days. He has taken his life seriously. So he takes it up with God in prayer. He cannot settle for anything less than God's best. He has to pray and he prays. Before the thoughts in his heart develop into action, he acts in prayer. He needs to know whether what he has is of God or it is of his own. It is the devil that will bring half-godly thoughts like how he brought to Peter, when he rebuked Jesus concerning His impending sufferings. Jesus had to cast the devil out of him. God never works in the gray areas. There is no uncertainty about His plans. His ways and plans are sure and perfect. His instructions are clear.

There is enough we have got to tell God if we consider Him part of our daily lives. You need not struggle for words, if you tell

Him everything you have in your heart. How long you pray? How often you pray? How intense you pray? These are all vital signs of your relationship to God. These all show how much God is part of your life. "He shall hear my voice." What a consolation! Not even once will He shun or ask you to come later. Every time you go to Him, you are surprised to see that He has been waiting for you. You might feel like, 'But God aren't You busy to mind the whole universe?' That's how much He values your relationship. He will hear your voice.

'Too busy to pray' Is one of the most shameful words found in the dictionaries of all human languages that exist.

Chapter 5

PRAYING IN
DIFFICULT TIMES

There was a couple whom I knew who were going through a hard time. They were fighting battles in many fronts. Having sensed their desperate condition, I decided to pray with them. The Scripture tells that we help others through prayer (2 Cor. 1:11). We started spending a few hours of prayer in the night once a week till 1am. During those days, there was another painful incident that happened in a family close to me. A child born preterm was going through a life-or-death battle. It was a heartbreaking situation. Physically they were in a great distance. We were praying about these issues during those night vigils. We needed breakthroughs that only the Lord could give. I was fasting even as we prayed together.

That particular night we were praying for this child with great burden and faith. I was asking God to intervene. As I was praying in the Spirit, the Lord opened my spiritual eyes. I could see a person close to twelve feet high. I observed to realize that it was an angel. The angel was about a few feet from where we prayed. I was asking for a miracle that the life of the child would be spared. As we prayed more and more, I could see myself literally trying to move the angel as if he had the answer concerning this petition. The angel was a huge figure and he was on his knees. After a good while of prayer, the angel moved. At that point, I felt in my spirit, that our prayers have been answered. I was reminded of how Jacob prayed in his desperate moment, and prevailed over the angel who wrestled with him. Jacob would not let go of the angel till the angel would bless him (Gen. 32:24–26). After this supernatural encounter I had, the very next day we heard that the Lord had done a miracle. The child was healed in a miraculous way. Everyone testified in the hospital that it was an uncommon healing.

I Am Not Giving Up

> But me, I'm not giving up. I'm sticking around to see what GOD will do. I'm waiting for God to make things right. I'm counting on God to listen to me.

> –Mic.7:7, MSG

Stick Around. Stay with God as Elisha was with prophet Elijah. Elisha would not mind going from town to town with his master even if it seemed meaningless to others. Only he knew what he had set his heart upon. It was the double portion of the anointing that the man of God Elijah had (2 Kings 2:1–13). They started at Gilgal, and went through Bethel, Jericho and Jordan. Each town they passed through has its spiritual significance. Even today God takes us through those spiritual spots in our lives as we choose to move along in prayer.

And we need to follow Him wholeheartedly. Elijah and Elisha his servant both started from Gilgal. Gilgal is the place where the unbelief and murmurings of the Israelites were finally put to rest through the pain of circumcision (Josh. 5:1–9). It was the rolling away of the attitude of Egypt which had been in them. At the end of forty years in the wilderness, they entered Canaan. At Gilgal, they were finally delivered from the shameful slavery of Egypt. After that covenant renewal through circumcision, the children of Israel never murmured under the leadership of Joshua. The only time that they murmured under Joshua was when the elders did not consult God and made a false treaty with the Gibeonites. Good murmuring! God takes us through Gilgal where He wants our guilt of the past and shame to be put to rest, that we may walk in the freedom of true sonship.

Then Elisha followed Elijah to Bethel. Bethel was the place where God appeared to Jacob in his day of trouble when he fled from his brother Esau (Gen. 28:10–17). When Jacob felt like an orphan, in his lowest moment, God Most High made a covenant with him by giving him a dream. God's promises are true even in the lowest points of life. Bethel is the house of God where you meet the God of covenant and He gives you His promises.

Then Elijah and Elisha went from Bethel to Jericho. Jericho was the firstfruits of the victories in the Promised Land (Josh. 6:1–20). As they came around the city 7 days without a noise, God prepared them through obedience. God gave them victory as they shouted at Joshua's command in the last day. It means to joyfully walk in obedience even when you don't understand why God gives you certain instructions. It is a level where you wholly depend on the power of God.

Finally, Elijah went from Jericho to Jordan and Elisha followed. When Elijah parted the waters of Jordan by his mantle, it was a reminder to Elisha about the power of God's presence (Josh. 3:3–17). When the Israelites came to Jordan, the priests carrying the ark were commanded to put their feet on the flooded river. When they did so, the waters were cut off. The Israelites learnt to believe and honor the presence of God. It is a level where you care for the anointing and the grace that you carry. You handle His presence with care.

The following of Elisha brought him through the reality of these experiences. By now, Elisha had gone through a great preparation in his spirit. It was not easy to keep going. But he never gave up.

He looked at Elijah when he was raptured. It was worth it all when the mantle fell from the chariots of fire and he received the double power. All along, Elisha never minded those people who tried to distract him. He pressed on.

So was Ruth following Naomi leaving her country and she received a timeless inheritance. Being with the Lord, observing what He is doing, listening to the words He speaks, accepting the change He brings about and pouring out your heart—these are to be done if you do not want to give up. "To see what GOD will do." (Mic. 7:7) Only those people who want God to do things wait on Him. Others quickly proceed by themselves to settle for less. To wrestle with God and prevail gives you nothing less than the best.

Wait on Him until things become right in your life's situations. They have to become right no matter how difficult they may appear today. Do you know why? He is God and everything has to give way to Him. He is Almighty, so there is nothing impossible. He is the Creator and so He can create what you need from nothing. Make the decision: Never to give up! Do not let the devil lie to you that it is difficult to find God. The devil is a liar. You will find God as you seek Him with your whole heart. He is waiting for you.

It Is Never Too Worse to Pray

> The LORD is good to those who wait for Him, to the soul who seeks Him.
>
> –Lamentations 3:25

The book of Lamentations is the book of utter disappointment and despair. And in the midst of such havoc is a prophet found interceding for the people and the land. There is no limit to prayer. Even when it seems that things have left our hands, and the damage done is irreparable, there is still hope in prayer. Nothing is beyond the reach of passionate prayer. No condition is so bad that prayer should not be done. No situation has crossed the brink of prayer. It is only the absence of praying people that makes God wonder (Isa. 59:16).

Every failure is rooted in prayerlessness. Just as prayer involves God and brings Him into human affairs, prayerlessness sidelines God and nothing can be done about it. Nothing replaces the failure to pray. Failure in prayer is failure in everything. It can never be fulfilled till people *wake up* to pray.

Jeremiah prayed. Daniel prayed. These men prayed when the nation of Judah had been taken into captivity. The Scripture records that God through prayer intervened in history and fulfilled His promises of turning the captivity of His people. He did them good by bringing them back. The prayers of men and women who sought God in the direst of situations never went in vain. Even if they lived not to see the answers, their generations witnessed the answers to their prayers, for God is faithful. Prayer *outlives* the man who prays.

In the midst of all odds, prayer still brings the goodness and the mercy of God available to us. How amazing it can be! There need not be any doubt about the effectiveness of prayer even in the harshest times. God through prayer can turn the tables around, change lives, and accomplish the impossible. After all, there is no impossibility with God. God never turns a deaf ear to the man who is prevalent in prayer. He will respond. We need to be delivered from showcasing reasons for not praying. It is indeed false justification. Get to pray. No quicksand can swallow up the kneeling child of God.

The Prevailing Travail

> Behold, as the eyes of servants *look* unto the hand
> of their masters, . . .so our eyes *wait* upon the LORD
> our God, until that he have mercy upon us.

> –Psalm 123:2 KJV

Waiting on the Lord demands time and focus. The word 'wait' gives us a fair idea that it involves time. While many want things to happen immediately, waiting is more than getting answers to prayer. It is building an intimate relationship in which you come to know God intimately—His pleasures, passion and inhibitions. It results in receiving the mind of Christ.

"As the eyes of servants look unto the hand of their masters. . ." It is intently gazing at Him putting all the craving of your heart in your look. It is a penetrating look, controlling look that will not allow Jesus to pass by. It is a prevailing travail that God has to yield to. There is persistence and passion in that heart that He cannot move anymore. He declares, "great is your faith", and performs the impossible (Matt. 15:28). It is the waiting that will not *exit* the door without the answer.

When Jesus walked past the blind man and people restrained him, his cry of faith brought his healing. When Jairus' prayer moved Jesus toward his house for his daughter's healing, an even more compelling faith of the woman with the issue of blood stopped Him and released healing for her. Are you a man of compelling prayer who wouldn't quit till the answer arrives? You need the Spirit to birth answers through concentrated prayer. You need an *untiringly* prayerful heart.

Chapter 6

JABEZ, THE MAN WHO PRAYED HIMSELF INTO BLESSING

Pauper–Prayer–Prince

Now Jabez was more honorable than his brothers, . .

–1 Chronicles 4:9

The name of a young man "Jabez" suddenly appears among the genealogy of the tribe of Judah. He is not identified with the name of his father. This reveals that he had a humble beginning. His name 'Jabez' given to him by his mother meant, "pain-causer". What a curse to be named by his mother that way! All these prove the fact that he was a not-so-wanted person by nature and name, by birth and being.

Growing up with difficulties, and at the heights of hopelessness in life, his decision to have a meeting with the God of Israel brought a sea of change in his life. Jabez prayed and prayed till the answer came. He did not pray and grumble, pray and murmur. He prayed till it happened. Though this is recorded as a one-verse prayer, this should have been the outline of what he would have prayed for years. As he prayed, God changed him inside out. God removed his sackcloth. He made a pauper into a prince. He was made honorable than all his siblings. The last became the first as he prayed. "So God granted him what he requested." (1 Chron. 4:10) What a testimony!

We even find a city in Judah named after Jabez (I Chron. 2:55). What an honor! From the ash-pit of shame to the gateway of glory–because Jabez prayed. Prayer is the power that gets the attention of the God of heaven. Through prayer, God can make the impossible happen in the lives of His saints. Heaven recognizes the man of prayer. Heaven is honored with such a man being alive on earth. Praying abundantly and commitment to sincere prayer is the channel for increase. May God help us be true to our hearts and to Him by depending on Him through prayer. It's His grace that can keep us in that lofty task of praying to victory, and praying beyond victory.

Destiny Changing God!

> and his mother called his name Jabez, saying, "Because I bore *him* in pain."

> –1 Chronicles 4:9

The story of Jabez helps us to understand how the power of God's mercy can take us beyond the agony of human incapability. "Jabez" might seem to be a sweet name on our lips today and some Christian parents so name their sons. But Jabez was named so because his mother said: I bore him with sorrow (pain). She probably went through the worst of her life when the baby was still in her womb, or she experienced an unusual horror while giving birth. A mother to name her child as 'pain causer' shows that she had suffered enough. She could take no more. She somehow felt that if the child being inside would cause so much pain, how much more she had to face, when he grew up to become a man.

Every one of his friends and family called him a 'pain causer'. What a pain with which Jabez would have writhed every time he heard someone call his name. His name was literally a *curse* upon his life. How miserable it is! But Jabez never gave up. He knew that God had an answer. He would not quit. His incapacity could never stop him from being the best. As he prayed, we see God intervening in his life. He was more honorable than his brethren. Maybe they had nice names. But God took him beyond the curse that hung over his head and the name he had.

No one can thwart the destiny that you have in God. Our God is a *destiny-changer*. Man's impossibilities are God's opportunities, if we don't give up in prayer.

The Door That Never Shuts

And Jabez called on the God of Israel,

–I Chronicles 4:10

As humans, we seek the recognition, approval and acceptance of people around us. There is nothing wrong about it. But what happens when we are disapproved, rejected and not recognized? It is here the problem creeps in. Our heart sinks into the depths of self-pity, even leading to self-hatred. When the feeling of low self-esteem takes over, it ruins a bright life.

Despised by everyone, Jabez should have been a heart-broken man. He went to bed every night with a heavy heart caused by disrepute. The only identity he had with people was a curse that his name meant "pain-causer". His life seemed meaningless. When every door has been shut on your face, doing what Jabez did is the solution. He didn't go in search of a man to help him. He called on

God. He went to the God of Israel. There are times definitely in life when the presence of God is so near us. His door never goes shut. Those are the times when our hearts are broken. "The sacrifices of God *are* a broken spirit, a broken and a contrite heart – these, O God, You will not despise" (Ps. 51:17). The faith-giants of the Bible were those who had their meeting with God. They were broken people who poured their hearts out, tore their spirits and vented their pains to God in the midst of their loneliness. He turned their impossibilities into possibilities.

God is closer to a man during his hard times. The reason being, the heart is humble, ready to believe, and the man is ready to obey. These results of brokenness take us closer to God. If you are going through the aftermath of a disaster, remember the Father-heart of God is closer to you. Connecting with Him now is the key for the restoration of a life that you feel that you have lost.

Pour Out Your Heart

And Jabez called on the God of Israel, saying, "Oh . .

–I Chronicles 4:10

One thing that yields profit to a man is to get soaked in the word of God (Isa. 48:17). As we soak ourselves in the word looking into the life of Jabez, we are moved at the truth that God regards the painful cry. Man is an emotional being. We are not machines. Many of us at the face of a discouraging situation, store up a great deal of emotions, which we want to pour into someone trustworthy. Keeping such things to ourselves over time may crush us emotionally.

Prayer is a beautiful channel ordained by God. God has made it a path through which we can communicate to Him all our needs, be it, physical, mental, emotional and spiritual. And God listens to all of those groaning with care, and He answers us the right way at the right time. Prayer is the way to release ourselves to God and to receive His nature into our beings. Jabez cried out to God in pain, saying: Oh. The word 'Oh' means exploding emotions. This meant all the pain of Jabez and all his apprehensions. God cares for us and so we can cast all our worries onto Him (1 Pet. 5:7). When Hannah chose to pour out her heart and release all her shame of barrenness to God, God heard her, remembered her and blessed her with Samuel (1 Sam. 1:10–19). When your heart is so overwhelmed, it's ok to cry out your pain to God, during your prayer time. He understands! Much of the psalms talk about the uncensored pain God is willing to listen from a man who prays. He grieves when you grieve. He weeps when you weep. He will comfort you in your distress as you go to Him in prayer.

Divine Enlargement

and enlarge my territory, . .

–I Chronicles 4:10

Divine promotion or enlargement is the multiplication that He commands into our situations. God increases the few things we have and performs wonders out of nothing. When God prospered Jacob, he said, "I am not worthy of the least of all the mercies and of all the truth which You have shown Your servant; for I crossed over this Jordan with my staff, and now I have become two companies" (Gen. 32:10).

We are born into this world limited in certain areas of our lives. Some even develop disabilities along the way. But it is not so that we should live all our lives with these limitations. God desires our increase. We can choose increase if we want to. God has put the desire to increase in every person. The baby is about a foot and a few pounds when born. But in course of time, it grows and grows that at one stage, it has already increased to many times its birth-dimensions. God wants to enlarge you. In fact, when He created you, He has designed you for increase and enlargement. He wants to give you an increase in every field: spiritual, physical, mental, emotional and material. If you can believe, God can and He will increase you until you are far beyond your limits and step into the territories He has for you. His ways and thoughts concerning you are higher as the heavens are higher than the earth. He has a future and a hope for you. Do not make the mistake of settling for the mediocre life. God wants your increase. And He will promote you, if you are willing.

He is the God of increase. His desire is for your increase. Believe it. Live with this vision. Run with it. Don't bow to the limits set by your family, financial or educational backgrounds. Don't let your mockers stop you from praying for increase. "Do not fear, little flock, for it is your Father's good pleasure to give you the kingdom" (Luke 12:32). Nobody can promote you the way God does. If He could make Joseph the slave to become Pharaoh's father, David the shepherd to be the cornerstone of an unending dynasty, and Daniel the prisoner of war into a great leader, He would promote you to be the head. You will not be the tail. Pray and ask for divine expansion!

"I Need You Lord"

that Your hand would be with me,

–I Chronicles 4:10

Jabez prayed sincerely. Random praying may not get answers at all times. But prayers that touch the heart of God move His hands indeed. It is praying for what He has promised in His word. Of all the blessings God has promised to give, the unique thing is His presence. It is the cream of His entire blessing. Before ascension Jesus said: I am with you always, *even* to the end of the age (Matt. 28:20). The presence of God is the very being of God that is made available to the children of God in an invisible way. Though invisible, it makes visible impact in the lives of those who carry it. Greater its vigor in us, powerful its manifestation shall be. When God comes into our midst, every bit of our lives falls in place. You live in the realm of the miraculous. When His presence is sidelined, we settle for the things that are lesser than what God gives. It is pathetic!

The precious of all precious things is the very presence of God. Nothing can replace it. Everything God gives takes its value next only after the presence we carry in us. Without the move of God's presence in a man, even the loftiest blessing will be nothing more than a lump of clay. It is worthless. But the presence of God in a commonplace situation will make life richer than that of the richest man. O, the awe, the splendor and the healing, God's presence brings! It melts every mighty mountain like wax (Ps. 97:5). God's presence is upon a man who is thirsty for His presence. He waits on the Lord daily to be filled by God Himself. He is an angel of goodness to many. His words heal. His gaze blesses people's lives and soothes broken hearts. Of all the mightiest blessings a man can receive, there is nothing like the presence of God. God is present with a man who carries the presence. There can be nothing greater.

Living with a realization of your need for God fills life with His presence. Just as the fragrance of the rose crowns its beauty, so the presence of God is the crown of all blessings in life.

"Keep Me"

> And Jabez called on the God of Israel, saying, that
> You would keep *me* from evil,

> –I Chronicles 4:10

The next Jabez asked in prayer was "protection". Protection is the responsibility that God takes upon Himself, when He is given the right to touch everything in our lives. Protection is a privilege that God bestows upon His chosen ones. What could be a greater security than to be protected by God Himself! God personally undertakes the task of keeping His children day and night (Ps. 121:4). He neither slumbers nor sleeps. Psalm 91 is a wonderful psalm that reveals the complete protection of God. Before we can experience such blessed protection, He needs to be offered the highest place in our lives. He should be offered the place, from where He can reach out and put His finger on anything at anytime, and even interrupt our routine, if He would choose to do so. God's interruptions are the most beautiful moments.

Maintaining the blessing is as important as receiving the blessing. Blessings without protection are like houses filled with rich things, yet without doors. Jabez knew the importance of praying for divine protection upon the blessings that he was going to receive from God. The prayer that the Lord taught His disciples has this vital phrase, "deliver us from the evil one" (Matt. 6:13). Do not take anything for granted. Nothing has to be smooth, just because it has been smooth until yesterday. It is the protection of God that is doing the keeping for you. Keep your protection through prayer. Jesus said, "Watch and pray, lest you enter into temptation" (Matt. 26:41). Watching in prayer an hour everyday is the key to walk in spiritual alertness. Pray for your protection and that of your loved ones and all God has blessed you with. It took the daily prayerful consecration of Job for God to fence him and his own with divine protection (Job 1:5–10). Let us not let the excitement of today's blessings make us prayerless, and rob us of tomorrow's glory.

Personal Transformation

that I may not cause pain!

–I Chronicles 4:10

This is the most important part of the prayer Jabez made toward heaven. It was this final part which Jabez prayed that carried the weight to touch God and move Him to bless Jabez. Many people who complain that they do not have an answer yet lack this very thing. When we have been praying, but still feel like hitting a rock, we should ask: is there anywhere I need to make a change? It is easy to ask the Lord to change our situations and people around us. The most powerful prayer is: Lord, please change me. When Jabez finished asking everything, he asked for a transformation in his very nature, which is the key for the answer and the foundation of his prayer. It gave purpose to the answer and revealed the motive for his prayer. Having named a pain causer, he realized that things had to be changed from the root where his nature comes from. He searched if something in him was the reason for some of the situations he went through. He cried for a personal change. God had to deal with the unrestrained anger of Moses when he killed the Egyptian who was fighting a Hebrew. God sent him to the wilderness forty years before He could use him. Moses evolved as the meekest man on earth. What a life!

Jabez didn't complain. He didn't find fault with his mother, father, friends or God. He knew the real change had to be in him more than anyone else. That is the difficult bit. But when someone gets it, the person can get to where God wants him to be. Jabez knew that even if he had everything in place without him changing, he would still be miserable. It is this final part that may be missing in our prayers, which prevents God from blessing us. We should never be ignorant of the reason why we should be blessed. It is important to know what you are going to do, when God answers your prayer.

We are blessed for His glory. We are blessed to be a blessing. God's blessing should lead us to a quest for more of Him, and less of ourselves. God sees the heart behind the lips that pray. When He can see right motives behind a right prayer, the answer is right on its way. God made it happen for Jabez. He will make it happen for you.

Through answers to prayer, desire a greater personal transformation towards godliness. The real blessing is not something you receive for yourself, but you becoming a blessing. Every vessel that God raised is finally remembered for not what they received from God but what their lives meant for others.

Chapter 7

HEARING GOD THROUGH PRAYER

We had given the deposit for the purchase of a property for the ministry. The seller gave us a time frame within which we had to raise the money and give. Then he would transfer the ownership of the title to us. Those were times of an economy downturn. We intended to sell a property that we had. But no one was willing to buy. The deadline was fast approaching. After finishing one of my overseas trips, I was praying at the airport lounge before boarding the flight. There was a lot of concern in my heart. If it does not materialize, it is going to be very difficult. When I got in the flight and located my seat, I asked the Lord to bless my journey. Hardly had I finished praying, that the Spirit of God reminded me Psalm 138:8, "The Lord will perfect *that which* concerns me." The words were so clear as the sound of a bell. I was moved to tears by this amazing word from the Lord. My burden lifted. I was giving thanks, praising and praying for the rest of my journey. After I returned home, nothing seemed to move in the natural realm. Doubts would try to surface but I was holding onto the word I heard. One day, I felt in my spirit, that I had to dig the ground in that land we wanted to sell. It was a clear direction in my heart. It was strange. I wondered.

I asked myself: Why I should dig? Is there something in the ground underneath? If there is nothing, it would be a great embarrassment. After contemplating on it for a while, I decided to do it in obedience to the direction inside of me. I asked one of our church members to carry out the work. After working a day, we could find no treasure inside the ground.

On the next day, two men showed up in my office. They were those who were asking the land earlier for a cheaper price. When I saw them, I was not so happy. But after a few minutes of negotiation, the same people agreed to buy it for a decent price that was sufficient to finish our other purchase. They gave a deposit of one hundred percent! It was a great miracle during a time nobody was willing to buy. They asked for the title registration after two months. Unbelievable! I later realized that when they noticed that we were digging the ground, they thought we had other plans for that place. They had become so desperate to own the place and did not want to miss it. The Lord made them run for it the same day that He could give what He had appointed for us.

Watching and Waiting

> Blessed is the man who listens to *me*, watching daily
> at *my* gates, waiting at the posts of *my* doors.
>
> –Proverbs 8:34, emphasis added

There cannot be a better description of prayer—hearing, watching and waiting. Prayer is hearing. Prayer is not bombarding God to somehow get His attention. How wrong we are if we do such a thing! In fact, our very going to prayer is our response to His call to come and pray. When we have responded in gentle humility, now it is our turn to carefully approach Him for the next move. The most effective time of prayer grows out from hearing God first. The word of God is the voice of God. "One who turns away his ear from hearing the law, even his prayer *is* an abomination" (Prov. 28:9). Prayer is God's ordinance and it is not our weapon to pound Him so that He will yield. Let it be told aloud: God cannot be pounded. So to pray aright, only He can teach us. We need to hear Him.

In the houses of the olden times, 'gates' were swinging partitions on the outer wall and 'door' the opening on the inner wall. The watchman and the door keeper could be two different people or one person doing two tasks. The watchman opens the gate when that the master arrives home or sets out. The door keeper is the waiter who serves the master. He washes his feet and serves him food. He is at the master's call. Meeting God starts with learning to watch daily at His gates. It is to develop a regular prayer life where you experience the presence of the Holy Spirit. It comes through seeking the Lord with all your heart. Carefully build your prayer time by going through each step—praise and worship, confession of sin, praying for you and praying for others.

Waiting at the doorposts is a different experience. The servant who decided to live the rest of his life and serve his master was taken to the doorpost and pierced through the outer ear. It meant that his ears will always be open to hear the master's voice and serve him (Deut. 15:17). Bondservants waited at the doorposts and fulfilled the master's pleasure. Apostle Paul called himself a bondservant of Jesus Christ. That talks about arriving at the place of complete surrender before the Lord. It begins while you are in your prayer closet. When you seek Him diligently with a surrendered heart to carry out His will, you'll surely find Him (Prov. 8:17). Our prayer time should never miss these two parts: moving into His presence and surrendering our lives to please His heart. It is truly a great blessing to watch and wait. When Mary was visited by an angel, he brought news that could startle any betrothed maid. She had to become pregnant with the Son of God before her marriage. She lived in a day where such an incident would be met with the capital punishment of being stoned to death. It was a test of her servant hood. She had the option to say, "No". But she said, "behold the maidservant of the Lord!" (Luke 1:38). That commitment brought her to the lofty place of being called: blessed *are* you among women (Luke 1:42). You are blessed beyond words when you are yielded to Him.

The Loving Relationship

> Whoever keeps the fig tree will eat its fruit; so he
> who waits on his master will be honored.

> —Proverbs 27:18

Waiting is keeping. It is taking care of someone or something. In the hotel, the waiter takes care of the customer. Keeping the fig tree includes watering, enriching through manure, pruning, protecting and taking care of all of its needs. It is not a one-day task. It is not an emotional decision although it may involve loving emotion to grow a life. It is a commitment that the gardener exhibits with a great deal of consistency. And the answer is clear: he shall eat the fruit thereof. No other man has the right to it. None else can stretch their hands to pluck the fruit in its season.

Waiting on the Master is intimate, sensitive and meaningful. It is a loving relationship. That is real prayer. Waiting means to wait to receive His burden, waiting to receive an answer and waiting to relieve Him of His pain concerning the fallen world. A fig tree does not talk how grateful it is, till the day it comes to fruition. The man who prays brings the Holy Spirit to expressive joy. He is pleased to dwell in Him and let His presence to flow through Him. God takes pleasure in honoring that person.

The Desire that Makes You Hear

> My soul waits for the Lord more than those who
> watch for the morning - yes, more *than* those who
> watch for the morning.
>
> —Psalm 130:6

Listening to the Spirit's voice is vital as you wait on the Lord. Waiting on Him is not a time to fill your prayers with all you want tell to Him. It has to include a time to listen. Greater the ability to listen to God, greater shall be the power of your prayers. Hearing His voice is the climax of waiting on Him. It happens in the stillness of the heart. He leads me beside still waters because that is where He speaks.

Before that could happen, there should have been conviction, repentance, confession and cleansing. When Abraham had done the socially acceptable thing of his time in bearing a son through the maidservant, he had erred concerning the covenant of God. The Scripture records God's silence for thirteen long years. God was hurt with the chief patriarch. He stopped talking. Nothing could have pained Abraham more than the silence of God. It is no doubt that God desired to see Abraham's repentance before the divine silence would come to an end. When God spoke to Abraham again, he was 99 years old. God exhorted, "I *am* Almighty God; walk before Me and be blameless" (Gen 17:1) God started where Abraham had left before thirteen years—to be blameless. Having brought about that conviction in Abraham, He moved on to establish His covenant with him. In prayer, we have to move sensitively to get to the place where we hear God and live under the blessedness of His voice.

Genuine repentance is followed by praise and adoration and laying out your life as a living sacrifice. This is true worship. As you have surrendered, watch out for His voice in calmness. Watch for His voice to come up in your heart. You need to watch earnestly.

Guard your heart from preconceptions. You need not be afraid as you come to your Father. Be open for anything He wants to tell you. Come to the place where your entire being is craving for God and your every fiber is hungry for His voice. Those watchmen, who keep vigil against the dangers of the night, wait for the daybreak to see the rays of the golden sun streak into the earth and drive away the darkness. We need such diligence for hearing God's voice. It is that eagerness to listen that tunes your spiritual ears. Pray as little Samuel, "Speak, Lord; for Your servant hears" (1 Sam. 3:9). You will hear His voice in the stillness of your heart. When His beautiful presence fills your heart, His gentle whisper shall replenish your soul. His voice brings restoration!

Recognizing His Voice

> Thus the poor of the flock, who were watching me,
> knew that it was the word of the Lord.

> –Zechariah 11:11

Recognizing the voice of God is the greatest boon someone could ever have. When you have it, you are blessed beyond comprehension. Jesus said, "My sheep hear My voice, and I know them, and they follow Me" (John 14:27). Many people struggle with the thing of how to recognize the voice of God. They are confused at times. Other times they doubt. They ask: is this the voice of God? How can I know the voice of God? No one can teach you this trade until it is learnt in the school of prayer, personally and by practice.

"The poor of the flock who waited on me" (Zech. 11:11, KJV). Your mental or physical status never stands in your way for waiting on the Lord. But you need to get to the place of poverty in spirit. It is a place where you reduce yourself to humility. In the Word, we see the prophet Moses who spoke to God face to face. The one thing we see Moses doing often before the Lord was to fall on his face. Then the glory of the Lord appeared. To prostrate is to declare utmost surrender. It is to tell the Lord: I am completely Yours. Reveal Yourself unto me according to Your great mercy. Spiritual hunger is the password to access the realm of hearing God.

Those who wait upon Him know the voice of God. You do not doubt the One whose voice you have got used to hearing everyday. Get your ear attuned by waiting on Him. To hear His voice as God's sheep, we need the heart to follow Him wherever He goes; we need the discipline not to wander; we need to love what He loves; we need to have a will that is completely made flexible to Him; we need to desire continually to live our lives before His face. We need to totally depend on Him for our provision, protection and everything else. Aligning our lives along these lines, would help us develop the sensitivity to hear the Lord. You shall know the word of the Lord as Samuel, "For the Lord revealed Himself to Samuel in Shiloh by the word of the Lord" (1 Sam. 3:21).

Understanding God Always

> And I will wait on the LORD, who hides His face
> from the house of Jacob, and I will hope in Him.

> –Isaiah 8:17

God had hidden His face from Israel—You need the grace of God to trust Him even in the times you do not see His face. There are times when you go through a dark moment like David in Psalm 23:4, "Yea, though I walk through the valley of the shadow of death, I will fear no evil; for You *are* with me; Your rod and Your staff, they comfort me." That sheep which David talks about is himself. After a bright time of going through the green pastures and still waters of life, the sheep enters a dark valley. He could not see the shepherd.

But he knew the shepherd's presence was still with him in the dark valley. He heard the voice of the shepherd. Even in life's darkest times, God is there with you. He is willing to speak to you. His voice will ring in your ears. He will never forsake you. He will bring you through to your place of enthronement.

In such times, approach Him with a heart that will be swayed according to the desire of the Spirit. It is good to have a pattern of prayer. But let not that pattern control how God wants you to be moved in prayer. Let your prayer times be real and genuine communion with the Shepherd. Does He want you to be grateful? Be grateful. Does He want you to believe? Believe. Does He want you to obey? Just do it. Does He want you to declare His promises? Speak. Does He want you to intercede for someone in pain? Do it. Such readiness to the Spirit's guidance will make you sensitive to the Spirit's revelation. You will be prepared to see the strength of God revealed through a word in season. It will be the rod and the staff that will provide and protect you in the valley. It will give you the assurance needed to trust God. Till that moment of breakthrough arrives, walk through your valley trusting the word that God has given you. When that season of dark valley is over, you will see the face of your good Shepherd once again. He will prepare a table of honor for you before your enemies. You shall be elevated for His glory.

Chapter 8

PRAYER AND GOD'S PLAN

It was November 13th of that particular year when my parents had come to the saving knowledge of Christ after their marriage. It was a humble beginning. My father worked hard to make a living. They sought the Lord sincerely. My mother was 7 months pregnant with her first child (that is, me). That rainy evening after supper, they retired to bed after praying together as a family. About midnight, my father felt as if someone was waking him up. When he opened the door, there was an unusual level of water surrounding the house. There was a commotion in the adjacent house. When he enquired, he was informed that a flood was on its way. They hurried to leave the house and go to the next house that had a high floor. Taking the important stuff, they walked out of the house. It was already waist-deep water. I remember him narrating the story countless times since childhood that even snakes were finding their way in the water. When they reached the safe place, the house they have slept in a few minutes ago had completely submerged under water. And so, they called me "Moses", when I was born because I was rescued out of water. It was the Lord who had sent His angel, to wake them up and rescue them that night by His grace. They had prayed and sought God. God had a plan of escape for their lives. He had a plan for my life. He has a plan for you. But it requires prayer for God's plans to be delivered.

In His Time

> Therefore wait for me, says the LORD, until the day
> that I rise up for plunder;

–Zephaniah 3:8

God works His purposes by time. Just like adding the right ingredient makes the recipe to work out well, prayer is the main ingredient in God's purposes. God has plans concerning the smallest detail of your life to the one you consider as the most important. This is interesting! We always see the difference between significance and insignificance, but it is not so with God. Everything about you is important and significant to Him. God had plans about the entire life of Joseph, the master of dreams. He was lifted up by the Lord from being a slave to the governor of Egypt. When we rewind the episode of Joseph, we can understand God's plans.

If Pharaoh had not dreamed, Joseph would not have stood before the Pharaoh. If Potiphar's wife had not placed false allegations upon him, he would not have gone into the prison. If Joseph had not been cast in the prison, he would not have met the butler and helped him understand his dreams. If Joseph's brothers had not sold him, he would not have landed in Potiphar's house. If he did not have the coat and the dreams, his brothers would not have hated him. If God had not favored him, his father would not have specially loved him. In all of these, we see God's hand. And Joseph was connected to God. God was with him because he was with God. What do we understand? God's plans included everything about Joseph, his opportunities and adversities, his significant and insignificant times. In the end, God turned every evil into good (Gen. 50:20). But Joseph had to wait for God's time (Ps. 105:19). The name Joseph means, "God will add". God finally proved His plan for Joseph's life by turning every minus (-) into plus (+). He turned every loss to gain. God's plan about your life is all-inclusive, your makes and breaks. He wastes nothing that you have been through. He will bring you into the fulfillment of His plan. How great are the riches of the wisdom of God!

When we have understood this truth, He invites us to move Him to His purposes by prayer. So let us not think that when God's time comes, everything will happen, and I need not do anything about it. That is the devil's lie. Throughout the Scriptures, we see many instances, where prayer was essential for God to move in His time. The Israelites in Egypt have suffered enough under the tyranny of Pharaoh that their lives turned bitter. God had promised Abraham that after 400 years, He would bring them out with signs and wonders from the land where they had been slaves. But it was the outcry and the prayers of the Israelites that made God remember the covenant He had made with Abraham. Then He came down to deliver them (Exo. 2:23–24).

Not Man, but God Made Prayer

Man is not the author of prayer. The very 'idea' of prayer is from God. It was God who came to meet Adam in Eden (Gen. 3:8). If prayer was man's idea, God could do His purposes without it. But God has included prayer as part of His purposes. Prayer is God's main ingredient in His recipe. Failing to pray is failing the purpose of God. Every moment you take in prayer, you are actually doing the high work of working with God to fulfill His plans for your life and generation.

> And I will pray the Father, and He will give you another Helper.
>
> –John 14:16

God the Father had predetermined that He would send the Holy Spirit if His Son would go down to earth and die on the cross for the redemption of mankind. After the atoning death of Jesus, the Holy Spirit was ready to be sent. But it did not happen on its own. Jesus knew that His prayer would be part of the Father's purpose. He knew that He had to pray if the Father had to send the Spirit. After obedience to the death of the cross, Jesus prayed. The day of Pentecost was the result of the prayer of Jesus. The disciples also had to tarry in prayer to receive the power that was sent upon them. Every promise becomes a reality only after obedience, prayer and endurance in God's will (Heb. 10:36).

Prayer is not separate from God's purposes. Prayer is part of all God's purposes. It is the main part of every purpose of God. Just like the most part of our lifeblood is water, so prayer is the foundation for God's plans. God builds His plans around the skeleton of prayer. God deliberately includes prayer in His purposes. If God's plan is like a beautiful car, prayer is the fuel that runs it. He has made it so because His beautiful plan cannot work for man without man having a vital *relationship* with Him. Let us understand that in all of God's designs, He has taken prayer into consideration. It helps us to realize that God would not do anything if we do not pray. God needs a man if mankind needs to be benefited. And He needs the man to first pray more than do anything else. Yes, service is important but not more than prayer. God's plan minus prayer is *disappointment*. God's plan plus prayer is *fulfillment*. If one thing would still work when everything else fails, it is prayer. How sweet is that hour of prayer!

God's Plan Minus Prayer Is Tragedy

> Then you will call upon Me and go and pray to Me,
> and I will listen to you.

> –Jeremiah 29:12

It is important to accept that God has good plans for our lives. Some of us come up to the place of believing it. But not everyone wants to do something about it. "For I know the thoughts that I think toward you, saith the Lord, thoughts of peace, and not of evil, to give you an expected end" (Jer. 29:11 KJV). Then you are instructed to *go and pray*. God wants you to go to the place of prayer. It means to forfeit anything that keeps you from prayer. You need to set your face towards prayer even if it matters sacrificing some good things. Prayer is the best. Do not permit what you see as *good* to stop you from the *best*. When prayer is so neglected, God is shocked to find that no one prays. "And *there is* no one who calls on Your name, who stirs himself up to take hold of You" (Isa. 64:7).

Are you motivated about prayer? Does the very thought of prayer—its reach and its sweep *motivate* you? Motivation comes when we can understand what God can do through prayer. On the other hand, the peril of prayerlessness should also bring us to our knees. Take hold of God and command the works of His hands. Waiting for something good to happen without prayer is no good. It won't help. God wants His children to be involved in active prayer before He would act for them. He would do all that He has planned for them. Prayer is part of God's purposes and plans. Never separate prayer from God's plans. When you do, you are getting out of the divine structure. It won't work. Move Him through prayer.

Have You Missed God on The Way?

> Lead me in Your truth and teach me, for You *are*
> the God of my salvation; on You I wait all the day.
>
> —Psalm 25:5

We have placed too much emphasis on the difficulty of following. We say following Christ is difficult and so is doing God's will. The most difficult thing is not to follow, but to lead. Following takes only one decision: you follow the one who leads. But leading is making decisions all along the way. He never asks us to go where He has not been. What comfort and strength it offers! When we start our spiritual lives, we are on track concerning the hunger for prayer and the word. But we tend to miss God along the way. We become engrossed with too many things that we lose focus. It doesn't help. To reach the destination, you need to find Him once again.

The Song of Solomon talks about the love that God has for His people. When the Shulamite was about to sleep, her beloved came knocking at the door for a blessed time of fellowship. Instead of being quick to open the door, she was making excuses. Her familiarity with the beloved, made her feel lethargic rather than longing for more of Him. She delayed. Later when she finally made up her mind and opened the door, the beloved had gone. We see the pain that she goes through. She realizes her mistake and goes in pursuit of him with all her heart until she finds him (Song of Sol. 5:1–7, 6:2). Opportunities may come once in a lifetime. They come to the praying man. He recognizes when an opportunity comes and seizes it by force with all of heart. Genesis chapter 24 is a beautiful chapter when a bride is found for Isaac through divine intervention facilitated by prayer. When Abraham's servant had reached the city of Nahor, he prayed for divine direction. When Rebekah showed up, the servant literally *ran*. Being the eldest servant of the house, he did not care how old he was. He just ran and seized the moment (Gen. 24:17). Then we see that Rebekah *ran* to tell her father's house of the moment of opportunity she had experienced (Gen. 24:28). Later, Laban *ran* to meet Abraham's servant (Gen. 24:29). Everyone in the story *ran*. Thus Rebekah was the answer to prayer. She was brought to Isaac without any delay. The chapter ends with the *mission accomplished*. Nobody missed out on God's plan for the moment because action *followed* prayer.

If you cannot recognize where God is leading and what He is teaching, then you need to *wait on* Him all the day like the psalmist. It is vital to keep moving as the Spirit moves your heart. The voice of the Spirit is not known by its loudness. If it were loud, we would not hear and survive. It is a still, small voice that you need to sensitively expect. The Israelites in the wilderness had to constantly fix their eyes on the cloud over the tabernacle. When it lifted, they dismantled their tents. When it moved, they moved. When it rested, they rested (read Num. 9:21–22). The cloud was their guide to the Promised Land. They just had to watch and follow. As you learn to listen to the guidance of the Spirit within you and act upon, you will see yourself walking out of your wilderness and entering into your Promised Land.

Waiting all day speaks of two things: *refraining* from work to be at the feet of the Lord, and living with an *attentive* ear before the Lord. The first is to have a special season of prayer which we all need. We need to set apart times: an hour of prayer to begin every day; a day of prayer like what Joshua and the elders did when they were defeated at Ai; three days of prayer and fasting as Esther and Mordecai; twenty one days of prayer as Daniel and forty days of prayer as Christ Jesus. This we have to progress step by step as the Lord bids us.

The second is the experience that comes with a sense of *listening* to God in everything we do throughout the day. He speaks through His word, people, situations and commonplace creatures like the flowers of the field and the birds of the air. May our ears be tuned to hear His voice!

Wait for His Counsel

> . . . They did not wait for His counsel,

> —Psalm 106:13

Counselor! That is His name. One of the most important ingredients for success is good and wise counsel as we engage in the battles of life. We need both good and wise counsel because one without the other does not help much. Wise counsel is to have insight enough to overcome the situation. Good counsel is that which is morally sound. Counsel helps us make great decisions easily and helps us forge ahead. We face a lot of decisions every other day and some are really critical. Doing a mistake could make life fall apart. We need counsel at such times.

God never forces Himself into counseling anyone. He also does not withhold Himself from a man who seeks Him earnestly. We can approach our lives many ways. Some make wrong choices and face consequences. Others take the path of 'trial and error' and a good deal of time flies away before they come to the right point. The best way to make choices is to ask the Lord to counsel us regarding the direction to take. David enquired the Lord about his decisions. He did not go by what he saw, what he heard or how he felt. In 1 Samuel chapter 30, we see the Amalekite army raiding Ziklag and taking away all the possessions, the families of David and those of his soldiers. They had burnt the city with fire. When David and his men came, they were shattered. The men even considered stoning David out of disillusionment. How painful it would have been to realize that no one stood by him! But he strengthened himself in the Lord. When he enquired the Lord, He told him to pursue the enemy. He promised, "Pursue, for you shall surely overtake *them* and without fail recover *all*" (1 Sam. 30:8). When David followed the counsel of God, he found his enemies and eliminated them. He recovered everything that had been lost.

God honors prayer by speaking out his heart on the issues of life. If you have not heard Him, wait on the Lord till He speaks. He shall surely speak. You shall know the Lord as your Counselor.

Chapter 9

PRAYER AND CHARACTER

What we truly are defines our *character*; and what others perceive of us is *personality*. Ideally both need to be same. In a world where camouflage is the order of the day, it is a sad thing to note that there are people who have two different versions and live with two faces. Living to impress others has got no say with God. Who we are on the inside is what really matters. While growing up, I was struggling with a number of issues. One of them was fear. I was also battling low self-esteem. It made me believe that something was wrong with me. But the truth was, I never knew my *worth* in God.

You may not be the reason for what you are struggling with. There is a root of the problem. It may be the words spoken at you while you were growing up; how you were identified; who they told 'you were'; who they told 'you were not'; how you were mistreated as a child at home, at school or among your friends; how somebody mistreated your family which has remained a scar in your memory; how people have tagged your worth through a nick name on the basis of some wrong you did and somewhere you failed; the guilt that has followed you even after you had confessed one hundred times. These are some of the instances that mould a person's character. To a great extent, what people tell you or how they treat you can become the foundation on which your worth rests. We become what we believe about ourselves. But our beliefs should be in line with who God tells that we are, no matter the present condition.

Though brought up in a good Christian home, every clause that you read in the above paragraph had a dent on my belief about myself. It put fear of many things into me, although I loved the Lord. Most of all, I was afraid of people. In the truest sense, I was an approval addict. I wanted to please everyone. At the end of the day, I neither could be happy nor please everybody. I was afraid whom I will hurt by not pleasing or who will hurt me. I read my Bible and prayed everyday because that was Christian practice. But I was a defeated person on the inside. This was my life till I was fifteen years old.

Then the best thing happened in my life, when I was taken to a meeting where I had an encounter with the Spirit of God which I had never expected. My life was far from such an event. It was the mercy of God which I am truly undeserving of. On that day, when I was touched by the Lord, I was convicted of my sins. Like Peter who asked the Lord to depart from him, I asked the Lord not to come to me because I felt so low about myself. But what I experienced on the contrary was love as an ocean. He came, and He filled me with His love and power. And I was overflowing with gratitude. For the first time in life, I felt complete. I felt forgiven. I felt safe. I felt healed. I felt bold. I felt that I was special. It was not that I was perfect. But I had received the boldness that God had accepted me. When that experience that lasted for about thirty minutes came to end, I was praying in a language unknown to me. It was strange yet beautiful. It was the beginning of a journey of love with God.

From that night, my prayer life changed. As a teenager who found praying for five minutes hard, I began praying for more than an hour and a half that night. The love that I experienced through the fullness of the Holy Spirit turned me into a bold person. Having been forgiven by the Lord, I forgave myself. I wanted to become what God wanted me to be. And it began to happen. My fear about pleasing people started to vanish as I desired to do what pleases God. Those habits that I was struggling with began falling away effortlessly as dry leaves wither away from a tree. The greatest boldness that dawned in me was the truth that God was with me, and that I can approach Him always and that He hears my prayers. This helped me seek Him for everything. Prayer was no more the religious thing I thought. It became a relationship. It helped me make unpopular decisions for the sake of Christ and tread the less trodden roads in life, which I would have never taken otherwise. I have realized that the more I seek God, the more He changes me to the one He wants me to be. It is true that if God did it for me, He can do it for you.

No Character without Prayer

> . . . He took Peter, John and James and went up on the mountain to pray.

> –Luke 9:28

Jesus knew that it was the day when He would have a heavenly vision. That pushed Him to go to the mountain for prayer. He knew that there would be no empowerment without prayer. "As He prayed, the appearance of His face was altered, and His robe *became* white and glistening" (Luke 9:29). Both the physical person of Christ and His garments shone gloriously. Transformation! Transformation follows prayer. As we pray, God removes doubts, bitterness and fear from us and fills us with faith, love and hope. As the heart is transformed, the face is transfigured. "They looked to Him and were radiant, and their faces were not ashamed" (Psalm 34:5).

The word of God is lifeless for a prayerless man. The prayerless preacher brings gloom. But as we pray, the Spirit of the Lord moves upon the hearts and makes them a fertile and watered ground. In such soil, the seed of God's word springs forth to full life (Mark

4:26–29). Without laboring in prayer, there is no improvement in the qualities that we carry.

Look at how Jesus viewed prayer. It was His source of strength; it was His way to fulfill the Father's business; it was how He would receive anything from God. Prayer transformed Christ the Man into divine likeness and revealed the pleasure of His Father on Him. "And a voice came out of the cloud, saying, "This is My beloved Son. Hear Him!" (Luke 9:35). The most significant sign of a man with a high level of responsibility with God is that he prays. He prays knowing that only God can change the human heart. No one else can take God's place to do His kind of work. God through prayer transforms such a man into His image. It makes me feel strongly that many disciples prayed for Saul of Tarsus. Then God met him and changed him. Later Paul and his friends prayed customarily in the river side. And God in His sovereignty opened the heart of Lydia, one of the richest women in Philippi (Acts 16:14). Intense prayer moved God to use His sovereign power not only to save Lydia, but also to turn her into a mission-supporter. Look at the transforming power of prayer! Let it be said with all reverence that even God's sovereignty answers the grasp of the praying man.

We need praying eyes to look to God, praying hands lifted to God for divine help, praying lips that cease not to speak the oracles of God and a praying heart that is ever set on God. A lifestyle of prayer profoundly affects a man greatly for God. God could use the disciples only after they had prayed. All their character flaws dissolved at the altar of transforming prayer.

Guarding the Sweetness of Fellowship

> I desire therefore that the men pray everywhere,
> lifting up holy hands, without wrath and doubting;
>
> –1 Timothy 2:8

Fellowship among people may sometimes bring bitter things along the way. We are not perfect people but that cannot be an excuse. We need to be transformed everyday. God uses imperfect people like us to change us. If we need that change, we need to open ourselves to the Holy Spirit. People who pray everywhere will have no time for wrath and doubts. The presence of bickering and squabbling reveals the deficiency or the absence of prayer.

A prayerless person is a source of one of the two things, viz., strife and backsliding. Paul clearly knowing the challenges and the troubles that would brew in fellowship made a strict law for the church Timothy was supposed to handle, "that the men pray everywhere." When the apostles were handling things in the early church and there was little time for prayer, trouble, dissatisfaction and strife loomed. They immediately diagnosed the lack of prayer. When they made necessary arrangements for prayer, the sweetness of fellowship continued (Acts 6:4).

When prayer fails, holiness fails. Sin of all sorts comes: the lust of eyes, the lust of flesh and the pride of life. Damage to personal salvation and the body of Christ at large are the bitter fruits of decreased levels of prayer. Where prayer recedes, there is no satisfaction. Complaining, grumbling, faultfinding, criticism and condemnation grow. Doubt gives way to agonizing breakaways, be it in family or church. Fellowship fails at the expense of prayerlessness. Prayer is the lifeline that produces and maintains the fruit of the Spirit.

Into His Likeness

> . . . And in the presence of Your saints I will wait on
> Your *name*, for *it is* good.

> —Psalm 52:9, emphasis added

The name of God stands for His character, character meaning, His nature. Waiting on the nature of God means to stay before Him till that nature affects us and transforms us. We need to climb the pinnacle of prayer. God Himself declares it, "And it shall come to pass, that before they call, I will answer; and while they are yet speaking, I will hear" (Isaiah 65:24, KJV). God answers before we finish praying. How does He answer? He answers by fire. He answers by glory. Saul the blasphemer was touched on his way to Damascus. God commissioned Ananias the disciple to go and pray for Saul. Look at how Saul was introduced by God to the fearful Ananias, "Saul of Tarsus, for behold, he is praying" (Acts 9:11). We later see Ananias' prayer made the scales of Saul fall from his eyes. He was a changed man. The demon of those days testified, "Jesus I know, and Paul I know" (Acts 19:15). Look at the high level of identity Paul had gained even in the heavenly realms because He was a man of prayer. Even the demons respected him. They shuddered at his instance.

Personal transformation is a miracle that may not always happen suddenly. But it is surely the result of learning the experience of waiting on the *nature* of God regularly through prayer and pondering over the word of God. You begin to come to terms with who Your God is, His desires and passions. He begins to touch you and makes everything about you pass through the transforming power of His presence. You are convicted by His holiness, changed by His love and transformed by His glory. You are changed from one glory to another into His likeness by the Spirit of God. The more you spend time with Him, the more His qualities are transported into your spirit and life. The likeness of God manifests in our character, attitudes, thoughts, words and action. The 'I' in our lives wanes away. He lives *through* us.

Chapter 10

SETTING YOURSELF UP TO PRAY

After that unforgettable day my life was graciously touched by the Spirit of God, which I narrated in the past chapter, I was delivered from the need of someone to push me to pray. I felt the love of God flooding my entire being. For the first time in my life, I felt that I was no more a stranger to God. I am loved and accepted by Him as His own child. Feeling so loved was too much for the asking of a fifteen-year-old boy like me. I started to experience the reality of the presence of God. I told myself many times that God is real. I realized that the Spirit of God was a Person whom I could always talk to. I began my day smiling in the mirror to tell Him, 'Good morning Lord!' I remember talking to Him everyday as I commuted by bus, by walk and even when I hitchhiked.

A powerful prayer life stands on one thing, faith. "But without faith *it is* impossible to please *Him*, for he who comes to God must believe that He is, and *that* He is a rewarder of those who diligently seek Him" (Heb. 11:6). Faith is not a feeling. Faith is the realm where God exists. He sees by faith, speaks words of faith and works by faith. We see it in the life and ministry of Jesus. Faith is produced when you start hearing the inspired voice of God from the written word of God. Just like greater knowledge about any subject matter on earth makes you an authority in that field, greater revelation concerning faith makes one a giant in the subject of prayer. The Holy Spirit is a Spirit of faith (2 Cor. 4:13). How does a person grow in faith? There are some keys which the word of God has to offer.

Slave or Son?

> For you did not receive the spirit of bondage again
> to fear, but you received the Spirit of adoption by
> whom we cry out, "Abba, Father".
>
> –Romans 8:15

What do you think about obedience of a slave to his master to that of a son to his father? A worker may obey his boss to earn his favor or for fear of getting fired. A son listens and obeys his father out of love. While the term 'slave' stands for fear and bondage, the 'son' is the paradigm of liberty and joy. When we go to the Lord in prayer, we need not have fear. We need not be afraid whether our prayers would be heard. We have been created as the children of God by faith in the Lord Jesus (John 1:12). We have been bestowed with the power of being called as sons of God (1 John 3:1).

The spirit we had when we were of the world was 'of the devil'. It was the spirit of bondage. We were under the ruthless rule of the devil, caught in the trap of sin and under the whip of guilt. The devil even chanted 'no escape' over each of us. But thank God, as we have been made a new creation in Christ, there is no condemnation (Rom. 8:1). No guilt. No fear. You have received the Holy Spirit, who is the Spirit of sonship. He gives you a heart like unto which Jesus Himself had. He is the Spirit of boldness and strength (Isa. 28:6). He takes away the stigma of slavery and makes you experience the 'son-feel'. He makes you feel forgiven by God, loved by God, accepted by God as His beloved, and adopted as His own child.

You never have to open your prayer begging, 'God, please give me something, or give me anything', but rather, 'Father in heaven, I'm here to meet You. Give me all that rightfully belongs to me in Christ' (Gal. 4:7). He makes you pray with the boldness Jesus prayed. When standing before the tomb of Lazarus, Jesus prayed to the Father thanking Him and affirming His confidence because He always answered Him. Having prayed such a prayer, He commanded, and the dead man came out alive. It is through the Holy Spirit we can have boldness to come before the Lord. As we make our petitions to Him, the answer is made available to us.

The Compassionate High Priest

> For we do not have a High Priest who cannot sympathize with our weaknesses. .

> –Hebrews 4:15

God has ordained various helps for us that we may overcome the hard times of our lives through prayer. Among those, is found the access that we have in prayer to our compassionate High Priest. Man is a mortal being with a lot of imperfections. But there is a verse which reveals God's love for such a frail person. Psalm 8:4 states, "What is man that You are mindful of him, and the son of man that You visit him?" God cares for us. Why is God so concerned for a frail personality? Because of the compassionate High Priest who is seated in the heavens.

Jesus is indeed the Person who has gone through all temptations, and was tested in all points—physically, mentally, morally and spiritually. Yet He is without sin. He is the true Savior and the Perfect High Priest! He not only has saved us by giving His life, but intercedes for us now to keep us from falling away (Jude 24, 25). Every time we go to Him with a sorrow-stained, temptation-ridden heart, He considers our frailty with compassion and lovingly offers His helping hand for help (Heb. 2:16). He sympathizes with your weaknesses and strengthens you with His strength.

> Let us therefore come boldly to the throne of grace,
> that we may obtain mercy and find grace to help in
> time of need.

–Hebrews 4:16

There may be times when the devil tries to storm us with self-pity, guilt and condemnation. During such times, remember that we have a faithful support in the high priestly ministry of Jesus. We can approach Him boldly when helplessness stings.

The writer of Hebrew strongly exhorts us today that we need not slither into God's presence with fear, but walk into heaven's throne room with graceful boldness, like a child going to a loving Father. How many times have you felt the prick of a guilt-ridden conscience hurt your faith? It even shut your mouth from prayer and made you close a Bible which you opened to read and walk away. It is so important for you to know that God never scores points by condemning you with sin-conscience. In fact, He delights when you begin to walk with the son-conscience, the consciousness that you are His child. Though you may not be able to fully comprehend the power of being washed by Jesus' blood, the simple way of understanding could be: *the worth of His blood is your worth*. How is that possible? When an article is auctioned, the worth of the article is that of the highest bid the last man asks for, pays and buys. We were worthless because of our sins. When Jesus bought us with His precious blood, we are no more worthless. We are priceless. Pinch yourself and say: I am priceless because of the blood of Jesus.

Made an entity of eternal worth by the precious blood of Jesus, your prayer has the power to engage all the powers of heaven on your behalf. When you are washed, you have the boldness to enter the Holy of Holies (Heb. 10:19). And there at the throne of grace that you find everything you need. By this grace, you come near His throne in prayer. Our Lord Jesus' continued empathy and intercession for us is our energizer that emboldens us before God. That boldness releases the grace to meet our need for the moment. We can come in boldness and pray.

Your Praying Companion

> Likewise the Spirit also helps in our weaknesses. For we do not know what we should pray for as we ought, but the Spirit Himself makes intercession for us with groanings which cannot be uttered.

> –Romans 8:26

We not only depend on God by prayer, we depend on Him for prayer. Without Him, our prayers may be sorely wrong. Human nature in itself prays against the perfect will of God because it is the nature of the fallen man. We ought not speak anything mindless during our prayer time. Vain repetitions are powerless. If prayerlessness is sin, praying wrong is equally wrong. But we are given the Spirit who helps in our infirmities and the High Priest who understands us and is touched by the feeling of our infirmities (Heb 4:15). The one Person the praying man needs to depend on to pray rightly is the Holy Spirit. For without the Holy Spirit, you do not pray aright.

Since prayer is high work, we cannot afford to do it wrong. Praying is wrong when prayed out of the boundaries of God's will, prayed with wrong motives, prayed with an unforgiving heart and a heart that cherishes sin. To overcome these and move ahead in prayer, God has sent us His Spirit. He fondly beckons us to avail His help in prayer.

It is because of Jesus we can call God as 'Father'. And it is because of the Holy Spirit, we call Him 'Abba Father'. In other words, accepting Jesus puts us in right relationship with God. Receiving the Holy Spirit gives us the power to operate rightly in that relationship. It is the difference between buying an expensive car and knowing how to drive safely. That is the reason Jesus instructed the disciples to tarry and receive the Holy Spirit. They were filled with the Holy Spirit with the evidence of a prayer language. There are many instances in the Book of Acts where people who received the Holy Spirit also received the prayer language (Acts 2:4; 10:46; 19:6).

There will be times in life when we do not know what to pray. In such moments, we need to engage the help of the Holy Spirit through the prayer language He gives us. The Spirit prays according to the will of God. The Spirit prays with such fervor that they are not mere words but His strong sighs and deep groanings. He prays inside the will of God and that brings the answer for sure. It opens the realm of possibility and solutions are released. All things begin to work together for good as a result of the Spirit's prayer (Rom. 8:26–28). Out of His prayer, is also born truth, love and passion to fulfill the will of God in our lives. Pray in the Spirit!

Prayer and God's Will

> Now this is the confidence that we have in Him,
> that if we ask anything according to His will, He
> hears us.
>
> —1 John 5:14

The right way of praying is to know what He wants to do and working together with Him to accomplish His purpose. Some believe prayer as an avenue through which they could just get whatever they want. It may not be right always although it is true to an extent. Prayer does not bend God to fit our purposes. Prayer bends a man to fit God's purposes, because His purpose is the ultimate. We could never do better than that. Apostle John makes it clear that we can ask anything, but it should be according to His will. The will of God is as good as heaven. So we need to ask God things from His will not outside His will. Anything outside His will is not good for us, and therefore it is refused for our good. Prayer is a process in which our lives are conformed to the wonderful image of our Savior, even as we pray according to His will.

God's will for your life is always the very best. It is nothing less than that. God wants you to be above and not beneath. He wants you be the head and not the tail. All you need to do is to receive the vision from God about what He wants you to have specifically, and as you ask Him in prayer, God will bless you more than you desire or ask.

Jacob was running for life. God gave a dream to Jacob in which a ladder was kept touching heaven from earth. Angels were ascending and descending upon it. God revealed His plan to Jacob. He promised three things: increase of his generation, inheritance of the Promised Land, and His unfailing presence and protection (Gen. 28:13–15). From that moment, Jacob knew the will of God for his life. It became the basis for his life, progress and prayer. After about twenty years, he was returning home. When he was given the news that Esau was coming with 400 men towards him, he was terrified and watched in prayer. He prayed on the basis of God's plan for his life (Gen. 32:12). He prevailed in the end.

So shall it be for you too. You might wonder: how can I know the will of God? Jacob did not have an automatic revelation. It was the consequence of a series of events that had happened earlier in his life. He was always a man who had set his heart on the blessings of God. He desired the ability that enabled him for the blessing—the birthright. It is the *anointing*. Jacob desired the higher things. He desired the power that brought the blessing more than blessing itself. And it pleased God that He revealed His plan to Jacob.

You can ask God about His plan for your life. He shall reveal it to you. He says, "Ask me of things to come concerning My sons; and concerning the work of My hands you command Me" (Isa. 45:11). One of the powerful ways of such seeking would be praying and fasting. Fasting silences the disturbing noises within our hearts and minds caused by worries, anxieties and tensions. As we fast and seek the Lord with an attitude of submission, anything that hinders the voice of the Lord clears off the way. When we pray, it positions us to receive from the Lord. Knowing the will of God and praying is the most effective way of praying, as it moves the hand of God for what He has already committed to do.

Are You Standing on Holy Ground?

. . . Prepare to meet your God O Israel!

–Amos 4:12

One of the glories in prayer is to experience divine visitation. Whole-hearted preparation has to precede divine visitation if we should not be disappointed. The farmer does not cause the rain. But he is prepared to use it when it comes. We cannot cause a visitation from God, but through our preparation we can be deemed fit for one. These are the days of the latter rain and the latter glory. God has purposed in His heart and promised in His word to show His glory to His people.

This is the reason why Jesus shed every drop of His blood and why the Father sent the Holy Spirit. God is going to sweep the face of the earth by His glory (Isa. 40:5). God's people, the redeemed shall be lifted up and established above all the people (Mic. 4:1). Preparation is what He expects of you at this time.

Preparation is being holy. To be holy is to be set apart. Holiness is the price we need to pay to see the glory of God (Heb. 12:14). It is dying to the carnal desires and worldly attachments. Before Moses could behold the glory of God in the burning bush, God commanded, "Take your sandals off your feet, for the place where you stand *is* holy ground" (Exo. 3:5). God was teaching Moses the importance of reverence before he could see the glory of God. Moses was a man like any of us till that moment. God showed him that it takes preparation to come near Him. The preparation continued for the different levels of glory Moses had to step into. He had to circumcise his children before returning to Egypt. There was no ministry without preparation. He waited on the Lord for forty days when he saw the hand of God carving out The Ten Commandments and instruct the law. Every level of glory necessitates the paying of a price. It deserves a life of consecration.

We need to remove our desires on the temporal things and come to the place of giving our total allegiance to God alone. When Moses removed his sandals, it was a picture of surrender. Surrender is a decision of will that has to be followed by the practical action of sanctification. We honor God by living holy lives. Ezekiel 38:7 exhorts, "Prepare yourselves and be ready, . . . and be a guard for them." You are responsible for your personal preparation and also those around you. Then you shall see the glory.

Effective, Availing Prayer

> Confess *your* trespasses to one another, and pray for
> one another, that you may be healed. The effective,
> fervent prayer of a righteous man avails much.

> –James 5:16

Healing starts with prayer, whether it is physical, spiritual, mental or in relationships. It takes praying with a pure heart, a forgiven heart and a forgiving heart. The first step in prayer is to get your heart right with God. Loving God should be total—with full strength, full mind and full heart. This means that our love should arise from a heart that is pure, a conscience that is good, and faith that is sincere. Fervent prayer is effective and it avails much. It is effective in the sense that it moves God to change people, situations and things. God has allowed Himself to be moved to change things when His chosen people pray. Elijah was a man with passions and burdens like us. That never kept him from prayer. In fact, it made him pray. He prayed effectively. His prayer made God stop the rain and then again it rained after a drought of three-and-a-half years, through his prayer.

When Jacob prayed fervently, the Angel of the Lord came down to be present during his prayer. Jacob did that which was neither permitted nor practiced afore time. He held onto the Angel. The Angel wrestled with Jacob to let him go. But Jacob was desperate that he would not. Even the Angel hurting Jacob's hip to dislocate it would have no effect on him. The Angel finally conceded Jacob's request and blessed the pleading Jacob and transforming him into Israel (Gen. 32:24–28).

The struggles that we have should be the roads leading us to bend our knees in prayer. Problems and programs should never be our excuses for not praying but the very reason for us to pray. There is no victory without prayer. There is no availing of the graces and gifts that God has for us without prayer. Preparation for prayer is so significant because without it, our prayer lacks power. Let us be reminded again that one of such important preparations is to forgive our debtors and be forgiven of our debts.

Chapter 11

PRAYING FOR OTHERS

Over the past years, my wife and I fast and pray on a morning once every week with some exceptions. Whenever we spend such time of prayer together, we begin with thanksgiving, then move on to praise and worship. Then we pray for quite a number of things including the family, the ministry, and for the concerns of the people whom we are associated with. It would be a time of supplication and intercession. As we unite our hearts in praise, the presence of the Holy Spirit would stream all over like rain. One such Monday, as the two of us began our prayer time by worshiping the Lord, there was a strange feeling. I felt my spirit getting distressed. It was not just an emotional feeling. It was obvious and real. I knew what it meant. In my previous experiences as such, I had learnt that someone whom we know or who is connected with us, especially in the ministry, was facing a tough situation. Many times it would be a situation when the person was in a near-death experience, in an accident or something similar.

I had the same feeling that morning. I paused praying and told my wife what I sensed. We began to pray earnestly for that person although we did not know at that point who that person was. We shifted to praying in the Spirit speaking in unknown tongues, as we know the Spirit prays according to the will of God when we know not what to pray. It was close to twenty minutes that the Spirit of the Lord was leading us in that prayer of intercession. Then I could sense the feeling of heaviness lifting away from me. There was peace in my heart. I knew the battle had been won. We thanked the Lord and moved onto praying for the other things. That evening, we heard a story that moved us. One of the pregnant mothers of our church had gone for her usual check up with the doctor that morning. She was carrying a full-term child. They diagnosed that there was no movement of the baby in her womb. When the doctor told this to the lady and her husband, they were devastated. She was advised to go for an induced delivery immediately to save the mother. They had to agree. It was right at that time, the Spirit of the Lord had burdened our hearts to pray and intercede although we did not know what was going on. What a loving God we serve! He cares and He is mighty to save. When they induced her, she delivered the child that afternoon. As they were waiting for the sad news, there came out a cute little baby boy who was alive, well and crying. The Spirit of God had broken the power of the spirit of death that morning through intercession.

God Forbid Us from Doing This Sin

> Moreover as for me, far be it from me that I should
> sin against the LORD in ceasing to pray for you;

–1 Samuel 12:23

Not praying for others is sin. Abraham prayed for his enemy Abimelech. Job prayed for the friends who misunderstood and hurled words of condemnation at him. Jesus prayed for Peter who would deny Him thrice. In the text above, prophet Samuel was not talking about prayerlessness. He was talking about ceasing from praying for others. It is ceasing from intercession. Not interceding for others is sin against the Lord. Those are the people in need, those who have been forgotten by others, but most importantly, your enemies and those who hate and persecute you.

Samuel was a man of prayer that brought answers from heaven. "Samuel called unto the Lord; and the Lord sent thunder and rain that day" (1 Sam. 12:18). So the people believed in Samuel praying for them, "And all the people said unto Samuel, Pray for your servants to the Lord your God, that we may not die" (1 Sam. 12:19). Prayer being the greatest help that we can do, we cannot deprive someone who is in need of it. God having given such a weapon of power in our hands, He cannot see us ignoring it when a world is dying around us. Prayer should not be restrained. It has to be utilized at full length. People in need should be lifted up to God in prayer. Any amount of lethargy, delay or denial is called sin. The fruit of ceaselessly praying for others is peace (1 Tim. 2:2).

> Epaphras, who is *one* of you, a bondservant of Christ, greets you, always laboring fervently for you in prayers, that you may stand perfect and complete in all the will of God.

> –Colossians 4:12

We cannot keep ourselves from praying for the ones whom we come in contact with. Epaphras had visited the believers in Colosse. He was impressed by their love, Paul writes about him, "He declared unto us your love in the Spirit" (Col. 1:8). He received their love. But he was not a man of good feelings alone. Prayer is more than getting impressed by the brighter side of relationships and people. Prayer is showing interest in the wellbeing of people. He was not merely excited about their love that he forgot to pray for them. When we only get excited about people and forget to pray for them, we let the devil snare them and make them fall into his trap. Always pray for the people of whom you get excited about.

Epaphras observed something by the Spirit that made him begin a labor for the church. It was like the mother at the beginning of the birth pangs. Intercession can be so draining. But the fruit is rewarding just like the mother is overjoyed when she sees the child. Epaphras prayed hard for the believers in Colosse. His prayer for them was concerning the will of God to be *perfected* in their lives. What a beautiful prayer that we can pray for our loved ones! He labored in prayer for the church. There was some struggle in that church among the people. They were living in and out of God's perfect will. He began to labor for them to stand perfect in God's will, as a woman laboring. It was fervent. It means that he labored till the will of God was birthed in Colosse. Though he was *one of them*, he was doing something none of them did. You can do it for your friends. Let us stop talking much about the bad in people and talk to God about them. He will do them good. He can change them for the better.

Confronting God in Prayer

> Yet now, if You will forgive their sin — but if not,
> I pray, blot me out of Your book which You have
> written.
>
> —Exodus 32:32

The only man who can get closer enough to God to discuss, debate, question and even dare to have a difference of opinion with Him is the praying man. All others resign to be 'dumb spectators' who think everything that happens is God's will, when they could have actually altered destiny through prayer. Truly the praying man alters destiny. Prayer shapes destiny. Prayer puts God to work and keeps Him working endlessly till the job is done (Isa. 62:7). Prayerlessness spoils the plan of God. God loves to be confronted by the man who watches at His gates. The heart of the praying man is *wired* by the thoughts of God and it *beats* in God's frequency. God *esteems* such a man.

God would let that man corner Him for the sake of the people, even when they have failed Him sorely, as when Moses interceded. Just see how much a praying man is worth in the eyes of heaven. God will decide the survival of a nation in response to Moses' prayer. And He would repent of the evil He intended. He would calm down and listen, when this man speaks. He would change His mind for the good.

He places him across the table and shares His secrets and discusses His mandate concerning nations with Him, as He did to Abraham. Abraham's opinion on Sodom's destruction was more vital to God than the reality of Sodom's wickedness. God would not, and very reverently, could not, ignore the *friendship* He shared with Abraham. Abraham could not be bypassed concerning Sodom and Gomorrah. How much power a praying man has with God! He is a covenant keeping God and He would not overlook a man who is active before Him through the covenant of prayer (Gen. 18:17–33).

He would let Elijah the mighty man of prayer demand fire from heaven. He would turn around the years of drought within a few hours when this man bent his knees to travail as when a woman gives birth. These saints prevailed through travailing prayer. They paid a high cost in their lives earning intimacy with God through prayer and then expending such royal privilege on intercession for the welfare of mankind. They would never take "no" for an answer when it comes to the destinies of men and women. God had to concede as He did to Moses. Even when there was no goodness in the part of men, He still decided to bless. It was the unrelenting grip of an intercessor who knew the power of a faithful and covenant keeping God. May I ask you to cry out: *let me be that man.*

Paul Moses C. Ratnam

God Changes Nations through Prayer

> With my soul I have desired You in the night, yes,
> by my spirit within me I will seek You early:

> −Isaiah 26:9

Waiting on the Lord is birthed out of an *intense* desire for the Lord. Desire as vehement as flame should consume a person before such waiting happens. It is a desire to see God in all His power and glory. It is a desire to see nations turn to righteousness and bow its knees to the one true and living God. Here the prophet's soul is filled with a great desire for God's name to be exalted and hallowed among the nations where it has been defiled. "Yes, in the way of Your judgments, O Lord, we have waited for You" (Isa. 26:8). He would like to see the judgments of God upon the nations. When a man begins to seek the Lord with fervency of spirit, day transcends into night and night into the dawn.

There need be no debate about the specialty of seeking God late in the night and early in the morning. Praying late into the night and early into the morning is giving God greater priority more than the usual importance in our lives. It is like the team of specialists performing an emergency surgery for sixteen hours nonstop that decides the fate of a life. When God could hear the prayer of a man called Elijah and change a nation, it was because of His zeal in prayer. He stood before God all the time because of his life of prayer (1 Kings 17:1). Throughout the Scripture, such compelling prayer has brought about mighty changes. "For when Your judgments *are* in the earth, the inhabitants of the world will learn righteousness" (Isa. 26:9). God depends on a praying man to *shake* the earth!

Finding Forgiveness and Favor

> If My people who are called by My name will humble
> themselves, . ., and pray and seek My face, . . then
> I will hear from heaven, and will forgive their sin
> and heal their land.

> –2 Chronicles 7:14

Boundless are the implications of this promise to be written into this space. But we cannot skip understanding at least the significance of it. God owns His people through covenant and the seal of ownership is His very name upon our lives (Deut. 28:10). God holds His people *responsible* for anything in the land, be it blessing or curse. God has placed His own people in the land as His representative and the land is for God's people to have dominion. This verse clearly mentions a truth: He won't destroy the land for the sin of the ungodly but because of the sin of the righteous—*prayerlessness*.

Before salvation comes on the land, revival should come to the church. The prayer of people who have understood their praying worth sparks that revival. To pray is to humble oneself. We raise our hands to the Lord God in surrender that we can't make it without Him. Prayer needs to be done in repentance and brokenness. God hears the cry of the land after He has heard the cry of the church. For the godlessness in the nation is allowed to thrive by reason of the prayerlessness of the church. Prayer brings the forgiveness and favor of God into our lives. When the church is forgiven of its sin of prayerlessness, the land will be healed of its sin and suffering. Let us lament over our prayerlessness till we are changed. Let us mourn on our knees for the destruction in our land. As we intercede, we shall be forgiven and the great Physician shall heal our land by His stripes. The medicine for healing the nations has been purchased at the cross. God counts on our prayer. And He will heal our land, if only we would get on our knees once again.

Chapter 12

THE INDISPENSABILITY
OF PRAYER

About twelve years ago, one of my friends had released a Christian music album. We had invited him for doing a concert. It was a beautiful evening filled with the presence of God and awesome music. I had kept my cell phone in the silent mode. After the meeting was over, I noticed that there had been quite a number of missed calls from our home. One of our friends who had stayed home had called us. I had a feeling that something was wrong. When we called, she said that there were noises heard from the room upstairs of our home. The stairs to that room was built outside the house so that it could be accessed without anyone having to enter the house. We asked her to remain indoors and not to panic. In the room upstairs, we had kept all the studio equipments of the church as we were in the process of shifting the church to a different location. There were a lot of expensive gadgets, including a video camera.

As we arrived home in a few minutes, we went up to check the room. Under the cover of darkness, thieves had broken in and the room was in chaos. Things have been strewn everywhere. In the midst of the confusing situation came the thunderbolt. The expensive video camera was missing! It was a wooded area with only four houses including ours. The rail track nearby facilitated the thieves to indulge in notorious activities. We were all shocked.

"What can be done?"

"Can we call the police?"

I told my Dad who was alongside me that we would not go to the police at the moment. We would pray. We prayed believing that God would do a miracle. To the human mind, such an action may sound irresponsible. We thanked the Lord that the thieves did not harm our friend who had stayed home. I felt in my heart that we had to take the matter to God who sits on the throne. When there is nowhere to turn to, we can turn to God in prayer. When there is no one to help, He is our ever-present help in the time of trouble. We cannot quit praying. We should not quit it. There is no other way of safety but to pray.

Later that night after everyone went to bed with a heavy heart, I could not sleep. I was heartbroken because we have really waited to buy the equipment. We shot our weekly television programs of the ministry using it. Now it was gone. I started praying with tears streaming down. I was telling my pain to the Lord. In the Book of Psalms, the psalmist always cried his heart to God in prayer. He told God of how his enemies despised him. He shared his suffering with God. Hours passed. It was 2am. I suddenly had a surge of consecutive thoughts within me,

"Whose is the camera? Is it mine or does it belong to the Lord?" It struck me like a thunderbolt. I had been grieving thinking that *we* had lost something. It was an eye opener. I was humbled by this revelation, and I started saying,

"Lord it is Yours. The camera belongs to You Lord"

"None can rob You Lord."

"No Lord. It is impossible to rob You." As I was praying, the eyes of my heart had been opened. Truly no one can rob God. He is God of the universe. As faith surged in me, I began to declare with authority in the name of Jesus, that the robbers who took that camera, their hands would tremble with fear from God that they will return it. God tells in the Scripture that He would send His fear to make the enemies of Israel tremble in battle and flee. He tells that He would also send the hornet, which is a symbol of intense pain (Deut. 7:20).

I commanded and commanded by the authority in the name of Jesus till I had peace. Then I went to sleep. I woke up at the hearing of the continued barking of dogs. It was 4am. I slept again. When morning arrived, we were thinking on what we could do next. My mom said that she would take our friend and walk into the woods behind our house to go and search. That was an act of faith by a woman of faith. Always our prayers of faith should be followed by actions of faith. When they went, lo and behold, there was a miracle waiting! The camera was found on a rock in the middle of a small pool of water. They brought it and when we checked, it was intact. What a celebration we had that day! He had turned our mourning into dancing. Weeping endured for a night. But joy had come that morning (Ps. 30:5).

It might have been that the thief had returned at 4am to keep it safe on the rock in the pool and leave. There was no other logical reason for the dogs to bark. Our God is a great God! He sits on the throne. He had turned the heart of the thieves to do the undoable. In 1 Samuel chapter thirty, when the Amalekites raided the city of Ziklag, they did not kill even one of David's family or people. Unlike the nations of those times, the Amalekites were known to commit war crimes by mercilessly killing the feeble (Deut. 25:18). It is interesting to note that they took the trouble of safely carrying them away. It would have been easy for them to kill the people and take the booty. God did not allow them to commit such destruction. David had a hard life like any of us. But he was a man given to prayer and faith. No matter what you are going through, remember that God has the *final word* over your life. No devil can touch you. No evil shall befall you. David recovered all. You too shall recover all. When prayer becomes the indispensable necessity of life, miracles become the order of the day. For God cannot fail.

Paul Moses C. Ratnam

To Stop Praying Is to Stop Living

> I am weary with my crying: my throat is dry: my
> eyes fail while I wait for my God.

> —Psalm 69:3

Let go of the idea of having some feeling to push you around to prayer. Prayer is the lifeline of the inner man just as breath is for the physical life. You breathe in health and sickness. You breathe in joy and pain. When the heart stops to beat, the man ceases to live. You have to pray even when it seems difficult to pray, when you are tired. Prayer is the way out. Lying down to sleep as the disciples did at Gethsemane is to be thoughtless about the consequences of such an action. Peter did not heed the warning of his Master to pray (Luke 22:32). Peter's prayerlessness thrice made him miserably deny Christ three times. But Jesus prayed in the agony of His soul and emerged victorious. It was the intercession of Jesus for Peter that made him rise again. Again the lesson told to them after Jesus had risen was that they tarry in the city of Jerusalem (Luke 24:49). When they did, they received power and boldness (Acts 4:31).

The psalmist had learnt the truth that he had to pray whether it was day or night, summer or winter. He had to pray in joy and in tears. The devil retreats over such prayer, and heaven rejoices to answer. Such prayer in the midst of trials torments the enemy of our souls. We need the conviction that prayer is not an *option* but a *necessity*. It is one of the vital signs of our spirit man. Sacrifice what you need to and get yourself back into your prayer-form. When you have it, do all you need to keep it, grow it and spread it to others.

Is Your Life Controlled by Prayer?

> I will wait for You, O You his Strength; for God is
> my defense.

> —Psalm 59:9

When you know God is your strength, and you know that the inlet of that strength into your life is waiting on the Lord, you cannot but wait upon the Lord. Is your life so controlled by prayer? Many of us know that God is strong and in Him there is unlimited strength. But we have not understood that truth to the extent that it *controls* our lives. It has to become our driving force. Sometimes we behave in such ways that we do not care to receive the strength of God. We think as if we have the answer and so we do not pray. It has to be retold again and again till we get on our knees.

The plain truth is: whenever we do not pray, we live by human strength that is *limited*. We are sure to run out of it. After it is gone, bitterness, complaining, weariness and the like come. We do not receive the strength of the Almighty God in our lives by wishing or wanting, but by waiting on Him in prayer. Just as there are natural laws, prayer is the spiritual law. As we need to obey the law to benefit from it, so we need to pray if we need to have divine strength. Breaking laws makes us the loser, and sometimes the loss may be terrible. But God through prayer works supernaturally for you. Angels get to work throughout your day in different places of which you do not even think of. Suddenly you stop, realize and find that things have voluntarily fallen in place. There is no confusion in your territory. There is beautiful divine order. You are operating in a degree of strength beyond your ability. These are some of the loveable experiences in the life of a praying man.

Should There Be a Better Reward?

> For evildoers shall be cut off: but those who wait on
> the LORD, they shall inherit the earth.

–Psalm 37:9

"Excellence" is the way God honors those who make the wisest choice of waiting on Him. The difference it makes is definitely seen. When people prosper around you, and the Spirit prompts you to lay down everything at the altar, do not be disheartened. You have to listen to the voice of the Spirit. Man's prosperity of today may not stay with him forever. Get to know the secret of going high by committing yourself to God. Staying high requires you to follow the Spirit in childlike need. That is the kind of need, how you needed Him when you first met Him!

You shall inherit the earth. You are called for inheritance. Greatness is not the *ambition* of the saint. It is his *inheritance* in Christ. God's way of getting to reach the realm of His glory is unlike what we are taught in human systems. With man, you need to do everything by your strength to get to that place. With God, it is He who fights for you, and does things for you. Your victory in God is not in sweating alone, but in your acquaintance with Him. God is not lacking power to work that He needs our strength. He really is in need of a man to understand His heart. God wants a man who cares for Him.

For many in the Christian walk, the first touch of the Lord, their first dependence on Him and their first love for Him has waned away as days had gone by. Dare not call it *maturity*. Real spiritual maturity is longing for more of God, to depend on Him more and to accept all His ways. Independence wreaks havoc on the Christian life. You can put spiritual life this way: as a child, you *know* none other but Him. When you have grown, you *want* none other but Him.

Go or Sent?

> And now, LORD, what do I wait for? My hope *is*
> in You.

> —Psalm 39:7

It is those who have come to realize the riches in the presence of God that dare take the time to rest in Him. Waiting is resting with Him till He sends you out. Are we allowing Him to speak? Are we going on our own without His fire fueling us? When He sends you out, you are no longer yourself. You are crucified with Christ, and Christ has been formed in you. You begin to think, talk, walk and do things the way Christ does. No life passes by you without being touched by the power of the Spirit.

Who holds your hope? You will be finding it difficult to find a time of prayer if you are of the kind who depends on yourself, your strength, company and knowledge. You have been seduced to think that everything depends on you. You cannot stop to pray. Beware of that life when you have become your "idol" and your "god". The more you pray, the more you want to pray. The more you pray, the less you depend on yourself. The more you pray, the more you are aware of your helplessness without God. You have learnt that nothing depends on you. You don't just say that you depend on Him, but you being before Him proves it. And He walks into everything you do.

The Prayer Times of Jesus

> who, in the days of His flesh, when He had offered
> up prayers and supplications, with vehement cries
> and tears to Him who was able to save Him from
> death, and was heard because of His godly fear,

> —Hebrews 5:7

When did He pray? He prayed in the days of His flesh. He prayed everyday. He prayed early in the morning. He prayed late at night. He spent all night in prayer. He prayed when threatened by enemies. Jesus prayed when He was the Son of Man hungry and thirsty as we are, and when He was tempted in all points by the devil.

What did He pray for? He offered prayers and supplications; prayers for every concern and need of His. He raised supplications for the pressing needs. He wrestled in prayer.

To Whom did He pray? He prayed to the Father believing that all things could be wrought in prayer. He believed in the omnipotence of God His Father.

How did He pray? He knew that prayer was the only way for answers. He had to accomplish everything through prayer. So He prayed with strong crying and tears. He did not just pray for answers. He prayed the answers down. He knew that the Father also depended on the channel of prayer to send the blessings to His Son. It may stir up our faith to realize that none of the prayers of Jesus was turned down ever by the Father. The one in Gethsemane was a prayer of surrender to the predetermination of God. He received empowerment through the angel. His was a life of answered prayers.

Why did He pray? Jesus prayed to be vigilant from spiritual death and decay. Prayer is all-round protection. Nothing else could keep you from becoming vulnerable to the devil and his devices. The paramount of prayer is that prayer prepares a man to do the perfect will of God, no matter the challenges.

Chapter 13

THE GLORIES OF PRAYER

Some years ago, something awesome happened during one time when my mother in law was leaving us to visit her relatives. She had taken the train to Chennai (Madras) in South India. It is a six-hour long journey. If you have ever been on the metro in Paris, France, it would give you a fair idea of how crowded this train would be. There would be all kinds of people including robbers who travel in disguise as commuters. Reaching the destination, she had disembarked the train. Upon arriving home, she remembered that she had a made a serious mistake. She had forgotten her handbag, which had cash, gold jewelry and her bank check books. It was awful news that anyone would hate to hear. She had left the bag under her seat, where everyone leaves the luggage. By the time they could get to the train, it had started its return journey to its starting point, through our town Trichy. What could be done? Should we contact the officials? We could do that. But there was no guarantee that anyone would retrieve for us such a thing. So we prayed to the Lord turning this situation into His hands.

As I prayed, I started confessing: I sprinkle the blood of Jesus upon the bag and everything inside. I was repeatedly praying the same. The blood of Jesus has the power to restore anything just as it restores the soul. It is the blood that redeems and protects (1 Pet.

1:18–19). After the prayer, I felt in my spirit that we would wait and not complain to the Railways at the moment. In the natural realm, it was a risk. But we chose to trust the Lord. My mother in law agreed. When the same train would pass through Trichy that evening, I decided to go and look for the bag. Faith is not a risk as some may feel. It is the victory that overcomes the world (1 John 5:4). We have heard of people robbed during their travel. But I decided to act on what we had prayed for. Waiting on the platform for the arrival of the train, I could not describe the feeling. I was praying under my breath.

When the train arrived, it was overcrowded. In the few minutes before it would start, I darted into that very coach where she had been and located the seat. When I bent down to check, what I saw there is hard to express in words. The bag was right where it was placed. I took it and returned with tears of gratitude flowing. It was God and nothing else. Nobody stopped me. When we checked the bag, there was nothing missing. God of David who made him recover all made us recover all that day. The blood of Jesus had covered the bag. And the angels of God had kept it as an answer to what we had prayed and believed. So shall it be for you too.

The Place of Prayer, Where Omnipotence Reigns

> But you, when you pray, go into your room, and when you have shut your door, pray to your Father who *is* in the secret *place*; and your Father who sees in secret will reward you openly.
>
> –Matthew 6:6

"He who dwells in the secret place of the Most High, . . " (Ps. 91:1). The blessing of Psalm 91 rests upon one condition: dwelling in the secret place. The secret place is entering the prayer closet, behind the 'shut door'. The place of prayer takes us to the habitation of the Father. The place of prayer is the secret place, unknown to human forces or the spirit forces of the dark world. Prayer time is when the devil is blinded that he cannot see the child of God. On the other hand, prayer opens your spiritual eyes to locate the devil's activities and destroy them.

The Father sees in secret. You are at His focal point when you pray. It is not just praying that suffices, but "dwelling" in prayer. Dwelling is permanent residence. Prayer sees God as the Most High—high above all other works, commitments and things that demand your time and attention. The reward is open. Consistent and conspicuous prayer births changes first in the unseen world, and then in the seen. The shadow of the Almighty is found there. As long as you pray, so long you abide in God's *omnipotence*. Nothing shall be impossible for a praying man. For God has ordained prayer as the ultimate pathway to possibilities.

One more beauty of Psalm 91 is that it speaks about the ultimate defeat of the devil and celebrates God's ultimate victory. In this song, God is declared as the only one who is Most High and the devil is the viper underneath *our* feet. The devil might want to challenge you in life's battles repeatedly. It is then, may you be reminded that when the devil wanted to lift himself to the place of the Most High, he was cast to the lowest pit (Isa. 14:14–15). The praying man lives under the shadow of the Most High God. The place that the devil's longing could not achieve, the same is given to the praying man.

Praying Well Is Doing All Things Well

> And when He had sent the multitudes away, He went up on the mountain by Himself to pray. Now when evening came, He was alone there.
>
> –Matthew 14:23

After a great celebration, when about 5000 men and many women and children had been fed with five loaves and two fish, and after a long day's ministry, it was time to be grateful, rest and have more power. Jesus had to do all three, and He did by praying. The people and the disciples wanted the teaching, miracles and food that He gave. They would need the same, tomorrow as well. Settling with them would deprive Him of *fellowship* with the Father and deprive Him of the *power* to bless people.

Knowing this, Jesus went to the Father to celebrate the victory, rest on the Father's bosom and charge Himself up with power to meet the upcoming need of tomorrow. Jesus should have prayed for at least six hours before the Father told Him that the disciples needed help in the raging sea. Jesus had the power to go and calm the sea. There was great relief for the disciples. There was reason for more celebration in the ministry on the next day because Jesus was charged up. Prayer demands your complete self to be with God. Prayer is one place to stop where you get everything. A praying man always has God *in charge* of his situation. To pray is to include God. Let it be said again: failure to pray excludes God from life's challenges.

Prayer Brings Angelic Service

> do you think that I cannot now pray to My Father, and He will provide Me with more than twelve legions of angels?
>
> —Matthew 26:53

The prayer relationship that Jesus had nurtured and built with the Father was commanding: *and He shall presently give Me* (Matt. 26:53 KJV). The prayer from His lips would immediately move the Father to send armies from heaven to destroy the planet. What power He wielded through prayer! Yet He did forego that privilege to die for you and me and make us righteous enough that we may have power in prayer.

The ministry of Jesus was full of angelic activity. There are few incidents that particularly demand our attention. In the wilderness, when Jesus had conquered the enemy by prayer, angels came and ministered to Him. How did they minister? We see that Jesus was hungry after the fast. They should have brought Him food and water from heaven just the way they brought for Elijah. It was heavenly bread and water that enabled Elijah to walk the terrible southern wilderness from Beersheba for forty days to reach the cave in mount Horeb. The angel served Elijah with food from another realm.

In the ministry of Jesus, He acknowledges that angels were ascending and descending upon Jesus wherever He went (John 1:51). They were constantly transporting miracles from heaven to earth—miracles of multiplied food, miracles of new body parts for those who came for healing, miracles of wealth multiplication like the draught of fish, and miracles of life coming into the dead with brand new body parts. Heaven was open over Jesus because of His prayer life. The heavens that were brazen above the nation opened because Jesus prayed.

At Gethsemane, when Jesus had begun praying, we find a heavenly visitor strengthening Him (Luke 22:43). Jesus was given supernatural invigoration from heaven by the angel that He would not collapse while He sweated blood in prayer. That strength took Him till the last moment of death on the cross. In all these accounts, angels were moving as an answer to prayer. Strong, prevailing, prolonged and persisting prayer brings the ministry of angels into our lives as it did to Jesus. Angelic service is not automatic but an answer to a life of prayer. For things beyond our physical presence and reach, we are privileged as children of God to activate the help of these ministering spirits on our behalf (Heb.1:14). They are ready to go, if we pray.

The Bible accounts for numerous instances of angels bringing

God's word from heaven, defeating enemies, providing direction, meeting needs, offering protection and so on. If you ask the Father in the name of Jesus, which is the name above all names, the angels shall get to work.

Extinguishing The Devil's Stamina

> Now it came to pass in those days that He went out to the mountain to pray, and continued all night in prayer to God.
>
> –Luke 6:12

You are faced with overwhelming opposition, and yet you know you have no choice but to move forward. You want to steer those who are with you upfront. What will you do? Pray. The One whom we call 'Master' did that. The anger-driven Pharisees were like ravenous wolves to trap Christ and end His work. But Jesus had to forge ahead in establishing God's kingdom on earth. He had no time to be wasted contemplating the threats of the enemy. He continued all night in prayer. Jesus would not relax His praying till the Father's hand was set to motion. God has promised, "and concerning the work of My hands, you command Me" (Isa. 45:11).

Jesus would not relax His hold of the Father. After such tenacious prayer, Jesus could have the boldness that frightened the devil and his agents from coming closer to Him. With perfect clarity of heart and mind, Jesus went ahead to choose the Father's choice of disciples who would represent Him and carry on His mission. There was no mistake about His choice. By prayer, He had the guts to choose the Father's will. Among them was the traitor Judas Iscariot. It was of the Father to choose Judas and give him the important portfolio of finance. Jesus was unmoved in choosing Judas. He knew that through prayer He would win the treachery of the traitor. Prayer makes the opposing enemy lose his stamina and you are emboldened to make God's choices. Nothing can stop you till you speak the language of prayer. If you do not quit in prayer, the devil will quit.

Where Satan Dreads to Tread

> Watch and pray, lest you enter into temptation. The spirit indeed *is* willing, but the flesh *is* weak.

> –Matthew 26:41

There is no situation when the spirit is not willing to get into a time of relating to God. Even the spirit of the wicked man is crushed in itself longing for a fellowship with God. But it is the soul that needs to make the choice of building that fellowship. The spirit is willing indeed and the flesh is against it because of its fallen nature. There is no holy flesh and therefore the mind of the flesh is death. Flesh needs to be *crucified*. Prayer delights the spirit, enlightens the soul and transforms the physical life. When Moses spent those days with God, He returned with a glistening face that drove people to knees from holy fear.

Some of the greatest enemies of prayers are sloth and sleep, misaligned priorities and preoccupation. These are the cunning agents of the devil to attack men in the times when they are alone. Not willing to pray will lead you into the jaws of the tempter and his temptation. When you pray, you bypass the devil's traps. You are taken through the heavily guarded highway. Intense prayer takes you through the path the devil dreads to tread. Temptation loses its power before the man who prays. Prayer circumvents the road to temptation. When you pray, you can never be tricked or trapped.

Jesus did not color the weakness of flesh. But He never discounted the power and light available through prayer. You can overcome the weakness of the flesh by the strength of the praying spirit. As Paul, we need to put our body under subjection if we are to pray victoriously (1 Cor. 9:27). Unbridled flesh that is let loose shall degenerate and become disqualified. Prayer puts the spirit in charge of the flesh. Even demons in the heavenly places saluted Paul because he had moved into the realm where the demons knew that it was no longer Paul who lived, but Christ lived in him. His identity was so powerful that demons terminated their occupation in people, when aprons and handkerchiefs that went from the body of Paul were placed on them. Such is the influence of a man of prayer in the spirit realm. When he shows up, every principality clears off the way. The kingdom of God advances in full power.

Chapter 14

IF ONLY WE DON'T
HURRY ANYMORE

As a family, we were on a courtesy visit to meet an elderly couple. Our children had come along. Our firstborn Joshua was three-and-a-half years then, and our second son Chris was a year and a half. We were already running late. Yet we decided to pray together as a family just before we started. (By experience I have learnt that plunging into tasks without prayer is like plunging into water to swim without knowing the danger inside. The time we spend on prayer is never wasted. It is invested. We not only save time, but also save troubles.) After reaching the place where the couple was staying, we were so engrossed in fellowship that our attention had gotten off the kids. Joshua had decided to take his younger brother to the rest room. In a few minutes, we heard the sound of a non-lubricated wooden door closing with a 'click' finally. The handle of the door had locked. Then there was a cry splitting the air. We realized it was that of one of our children. When I rushed, I could not believe what I saw. Chris had put his tiny right hand into the hinge of that massive door and Joshua had closed the door innocently. It was a terrible sight. I was shattered to think what I would see when I open the door. Is it going to be a finger-less tiny hand or a little hand with fractured fingers?

Holding my heart I did open the door. It was a miracle. The hand of Chris was whole! We calmed him down putting his hand under running water. Except a small scratch, there was no other wound. He did not even require a doctor's visit. God had heard our prayers for protection. When I later examined the door, it puzzled me because there was no way his hand could have been saved unless an angel had covered his hand. As I write this, Chris is a budding drummer for Jesus.

Final Words on Prayer

> But they constrained Him, saying, "Abide with us,
> for it is toward evening, and the day is far spent."
> And He went in to stay with them.

> –Luke 24:29

"Abide with us". Yes, Jesus yielded to their constraint. He accepted their invitation to go in to abide with them not because the day was far spent, but He *longed* to be in the company of His own. Nothing kept Him from breaking His journey although He was now the Risen Lord with more things to accomplish before His ascension to the Father. In fact, He looked forward to being with them. It was His longing that they would invite Him. Not that He needed rest but that He wanted to reveal to them that He was risen and alive. Therefore "He indicated that He would have gone farther" (Luke 24:28). O, the Master's tender heart!

He longs for the warmth of our fellowship. He wanted them to fondly remember and thoughtfully invite Him to *commune* with them. He would have been grieved had they failed inviting Him that evening. And they would have missed forever the opening of their eyes to see their glorified Lord at such proximity. There are times when a divine visitation is so near. How much we lose by being in hurry and leading busy lives? We cannot afford to lose the very purpose of our lives by feeling that we have no time for prayer. He is and could be the only source, motivation and direction of our lives. "He went in to stay with them" (Luke 24:29). He wants to stay with you. It would be our gross ignorance to think that we tarry for Him when He has a heart that longs to tarry with us. If only we don't hurry anymore—

Watching for the Master and Being in Touch

> Praying always with all prayer and supplication in the Spirit, being watchful to this end with all perseverance and supplication for all the saints

> –Ephesians 6:18

Ephesians 6 contains the armory of God. The apostle Paul discloses the unseen world, its organized structure and its activity. The *day of evil* has to be faced and overcome. We are not warring against flesh and blood but with the wickedness of the spirit forces. The least of slackness on our part may not be wise. He talks about the weapons that we need to overcome the attacks of the devil. His attacks are fiery darts, not just darts. They will kill, explode with fire and destroy.

Our weapons are mentioned—a life which heralds truth, a mind overflowing with the hope of salvation, a heart vibrant with the readiness of the gospel, a spirit hungry for the inspired word, a tongue professing the imputed righteousness of Christ, and the walk of active faith. Then something else is mentioned. It is not a weapon, because the weapons mentioned above are complete. He mentions prayer as the watchfulness of the warrior. A sleeping warrior with all armor is easy prey. A sleeping lion has buried its power. It is prayer that gives life to the full armor of God.

Prayer is the alertness of the warrior in the battlefield. It is the antenna that connects him with the general. Prayer should be done always: with all manner of praying, be it supplications or wrestling with tears, strong cries or silent vehemence. Prayer needs to be done with perseverance till the answer arrives and even beyond. Answers need to be maintained through prayer. We need to pray not only for ourselves, but also for all the co-soldiers in the kingdom. The entire purpose of being in God's army is not for us, but for God and His people. It is to save those who have been lost into the enemy's camp. Be in full touch with the Master. Prayer along with the armor of God helps us fulfill the *rescue mission* for souls.

The Lesson to be Taught More Than a Million Times

Pray without ceasing,

–1 Thessalonians 5:17

Having told this a million times, it still needs to be told another. The truth is still fresh, impressive and important. There cannot be the least leanness on this matter. It cannot be taken for granted that people know it. It has to be pressed into hearts whether they know it or not. This is the reason for Jesus to talk about it repetitively and the Bible to speak it countless times. This has to be preached, taught and practiced again and again. So should also be the people warned against the peril of prayerlessness repeatedly till prayer rules the lives of saints and servants alike.

The final note of Paul to the saints in Thessalonica: He was writing to them asking them to comfort, to edify, to love one another, to discern, to rejoice and not to be stiff-necked to the Holy Spirit. But underlying all these virtues is the virtue of prayer. When prayer goes, all of these go. Prayer gives the Holy Spirit room to work. The first lesson taught to a believer should be prayer. And so it should be in the everyday making of the saint.

When the people of Israel were facing the Philistines, they asked Samuel to cease not to cry out for them (1 Sam. 7:8). Samuel decided that day that he would never cease praying for Israel the rest of his life (1 Sam. 12:23). Even when Saul sinned against God, Samuel mourned before God all night and God had to intervene to stop Samuel's prayer (1 Sam. 15:11–35). Elisha was the man with the double-portion anointing. He was a prophet with a ceaseless, guaranteed prayer life that the king of Israel called him as the *chariots and horsemen* of Israel. His life and ministry sent chills down the spines of the enemies of Israel. His prayer lived beyond his time that a dead man came to life when the corpse touched Elisha's dry bones (2 Kings 13:21). When the praying man has gone, his prayer lives on-

About The Author

Paul Moses C. Ratnam is the pastor and co-founder of the Fountain of Compassion Church in Trichy, South India. He is also a mentor and coach to a scores of upcoming ministers and kingdom-minded entrepreneurs. He has been serving the Lord passionately for the past 20 years as a songwriter, worship leader, conference speaker and author. He hails from a lineage of missionaries and pastors.

During his childhood days, the lives of his father and mother had been an inspiration to him as they served God in spite of working in secular jobs. After a miraculous rescue prior to his birth, his parents dedicated him for the work of the Lord.

Though his spiritual life was tossed up and down, the Lord gave him a powerful visitation when he was fifteen. He owes that moment to the grace of God and the prayer life of his mother. As a result of the experience, a closer walk with the Lord began to unfold. Spending hours on his knees early in the morning and late at nights became a routine. It was at that time the Lord released the grace of songwriting upon him. He has written more than 50 songs and has released eight albums of live praise and worship music, in which he leads congregations into powerful worship sessions. One of his songs *"Um Naamam Vazhga Raja (Hallowed be Your Name)"* is sung throughout the Indian Tamil churches across the world.

Finishing his school as a gold medalist, he went onto pursue bachelors degree in electronics and communication engineering. During the years at the university, he used to spend times in prayer and meditation upon the word under the shade of a tree. It was there that the Lord equipped him with the grace to interpret the word and teach it, which resulted in leading his friends to the saving knowledge of Christ during those youth days.

When he desired to pursue higher studies, the call from the Lord came in a strong way, that he discontinued his Masters and took up the mantle of teaching the word and leading people into worship through empowerment sessions known as *Glory Conferences* across India and the globe.

He has written about 50 booklets on different topics including, *Exposing Fear And Eradicating It, You Want God To Change His Mind? Refresh Your Praise Memory, How To Handle Your Victories? The Answered Prayer* and *Lord Change Me Today (annual daily meditations)*. His weekly television broadcast has been a voice of hope to many in the Indian subcontinent. He and his wife Preetha are blessed with three energetic children, Joshua, Chris and Jeduthun. Together they make their home in Trichy, South India. To know more about the author and his ministry, please visit www.fountainofcompassion.org.

Printed in the United States
By Bookmasters